BEHAVIOR THERAPY
IN CLINICAL PRACTICE

BEHAVIOR THERAPY
IN CLINICAL PRACTICE

Decision Making, Procedure and Outcome

By

ERNEST G. POSER, Ph.D.

Professor of Psychology
McGill University
and Director, Behavior Therapy Unit
Douglas Hospital Centre
Montreal, Quebec, Canada

With a Foreword by

H. J. Eysenck, Ph.D., D.Sc.

Institute of Psychiatry
Maudsley Hospital
London, England

CHARLES C THOMAS • PUBLISHER
Springfield • Illinois • U.S.A.

Published and Distributed Throughout the World by
CHARLES C THOMAS ● PUBLISHER
Bannerstone House
301-327 East Lawrence Avenue, Springfield, Illinois, U.S.A.

© *1977, by* CHARLES C THOMAS ● PUBLISHER
ISBN 0-398-03643-8
Library of Congress Catalog Card Number: 76-57248

With **THOMAS BOOKS** *careful attention is given to all details of
manufacturing and design. It is the Publisher's desire to present books that
are satisfactory as to their physical qualities and artistic possibilities and
appropriate for their particular use.* **THOMAS BOOKS** *will be true to those
laws of quality that assure a good name and good will.*

Printed in the United States of America
R-1

Library of Congress Cataloging in Publication Data

Poser, Ernest G.
Behavior therapy in clinical practice.

Bibliography: p.
Includes index.
1. Behavior therapy. I. Title.
RC489.B4P67   616.8'914   76-57248

**TO JUTTA
WHOSE GENTLE USE OF
CONTINGENT POSITIVE REINFORCEMENT
HELPED AT ALL STAGES OF GETTING
THIS BOOK OFF THE PRESS**

FOREWORD

THE phenomenal rise of behaviour therapy in recent years has been widely documented; in a dozen years or so the number of publications concerning this method of treatment has risen from almost zero to equal and even surpass that devoted to psychoanalysis. Yet there are many misconceptions about behaviour therapy, even among practitioners. It is widely believed that the methods subsumed under this heading only apply to simple phobias; nothing could be less true. Simple phobias are rather rare and only make up a very small proportion of the cases seen by behaviour therapists. It is also widely believed that behaviour therapy works rather like a penny-in-the-slot machine — you put in desensitization, and out comes the cure. This is equally unrealistic. Every patient or client presents the therapist with a problem; to solve this problem the therapist is required to formulate hypotheses, test these in terms of therapeutic intervention, and change them when they are disconfirmed by the actual outcome of his intervention. Behaviour therapy is applied science; like all applied science it requires in its successful practitioners more than just a firm knowledge of scientific theory. Experience, common sense, intuition, responsiveness to new observations, humility — the list of ideal requirements is endless, and few therapists, of course, measure up to it. Nevertheless, the record of behaviour therapy in terms of treatment success has been excellent, even though many practitioners have been self-taught; even though the methods used are hardly out of their teens; and even though few therapists have had time to acquire that long-term experience which is so important in the applied field.

What is perhaps most to the credit of behaviour therapy is the fact that more than any other school it has been crucially concerned with the outcome problem. Psychoanalysis and other psychotherapeutic schools devote most of their attention to the *process* of therapy and show little concern over *outcome;* yet this is the one aspect of therapy which is of major concern to the patient, and which determines crucially the value of treatment to him. There are many excuses for failure, but there is no substitute for concentration on the outcome of treatment; if we do not do better than chance, i.e. if our treatment does not work better than spontaneous remission, then the patient is wasting his time and money, and should not be asked to undergo the treatment at all. Even after three quarters of a century of psychoanalysis, we still lack any evidence of therapeutic success for this method of treatment; fortunately we do not lack such evidence for behaviour therapy.

There are many text-books of behaviour therapy; these set out the principles, but they do not usually give any impression of what treatment is like in detail, what happens during treatment, or what determines the therapist's choice of treatment. Professor Poser has filled a gap by illustrating the course of behaviour therapy through a series of well-chosen examples culled from his own extensive practice; additionally, these cases have the advantage of long-continued follow-up. The importance of such follow-up cannot be exaggerated; many patients seem to recover on the up-swing of their cyclic disorders, only to slip back into despondency shortly after being dismissed as "cured" by their therapists. If lack of concern over the outcome is one black mark in the book of psychotherapy, failure of extensive follow-up research is another, not unconnected; outcome means not only the immediate situation at the end of therapy, but also what happens afterwards. The extreme youth of behaviour therapy has not allowed its practitioners to carry out as much follow-up work as one would like to see; Professor Poser has set an example which it is hoped that many other behaviour therapists will follow.

This book should be of great interest to all psychiatrists and clinical psychologists who have used some of the methods of behaviour therapy, or have felt tempted to use them; it gives a clear picture of just what treatment looks like from the point of view of the practitioner — and what it does to the patient! It is so clearly written, and so free from jargon, that even the intelligent layman should be able to understand it; indeed, anyone interested in the vagaries of life could with advantage read through these histories of maladaptive emotional experiences and faulty adjustments. *Behavior Therapy in Clinical Practice* constitutes an important addition to the clinician's book shelf; it is unique in the contribution it makes, and should be widely read.

H. J. Eysenck, Ph.D., D.Sc.
London, England

PREFACE

MANY informative books have appeared on behavior modification in recent years. Some of these dealt more or less exclusively with its theoretical foundations; others undertook to explicate new methods of behavior change. Only few writers have so far attempted to bring together theory and practice, as these interact, in the problem solving and decision making of behaviorally oriented clinicians in their daily work.

What happens when someone requests a behavior change? What are the criteria whereby one determines whether such a request should be accepted or rejected? If accepted, how does a change agent reformulate the presenting problem in behavioral terms? What techniques are there for the measurement and evaluation of deviant behavior? How does one choose between the ever-increasing welter of remedial methods; who should implement them and when should a particular mode of intervention be changed or terminated? To what extent can those in need of behavior modification participate in the process as their own change agents and how does one involve them, and significant others in their social environment, as monitors of behavior change? Once a behavior has been modified, what follow-up procedures are currently available and how can these be exploited to yield new theoretical insights and better techniques?

These are some of the questions to which this book addresses itself, not in the context of generalized principles — for these largely remain to be elaborated — but by way of specific examples culled from case material dealt with in a variety of behavior therapy settings. Most of the cases were seen at the Behavior Therapy Teaching Unit at Douglas Hospital in Montreal. As one of the first clinical treatment and training facilities of its kind, that Unit provided a unique opportunity for the longitudinal study of many diverse behavior problems. The majority of cases reported were followed up from five to ten years, making it possible to gain some perspective on the outcome of behavior therapy with clients sufficiently impaired to require hospitalization.

The cases cited in this volume were not randomly selected. They were chosen to represent as wide a choice of problems, techniques, successes, and failures as the scope of this book would permit. Priority for inclusion was given to those cases for which long-term follow-up data were obtainable.

ACKNOWLEDGMENTS

A NEW treatment facility such as the Behavior Therapy Unit at Douglas Hospital could not have been established without the help of many colleagues representing various mental health professions. Particular thanks are due to Dr. Henry B. Durost, former Executive Director of Douglas Hospital, whose active support and administrative vigour helped overcome the obstacles invariably associated with a new venture of this kind. His successor, Dr. Gaston P. Harnois, sponsored the enlargement of the Unit and extension of behavior therapy services to other areas of the Hospital. Most of all I am indebted to those colleagues, graduate students and members of allied disciplines whose cooperation enabled the Unit to achieve what impact it has had on the teaching of behavior therapy. Foremost among these were Drs. Beatrice Ashem, Saul Miller, John Raeburn, and Kai Thio. Ms. A. Earthrowl, R.N. pioneered the establishment of a nursing service for behavior therapy, and her successor Ms. Joan Soler, R. N. further developed this new branch of nursing education. To them, and many others who shared in the work described in these pages, this book is gratefully dedicated.

I also acknowledge with thanks some helpful suggestions made by Drs. Joseph Cautela and John Wright who read an early draft of the manuscript. For the collating of references and much painstaking work on preparation of the final manuscript I am indebted to Olga Heath, and to Ms. Kuenzi, Jacqui Penson and Glenda Coiteux for their able secretarial assistance.

Finally the author wishes to record his thanks to the Canada Council for a Leave Fellowship while this book was in preparation and to the Canadian Department of Health and Welfare for providing Grant No. 604-7-652 in support of follow-up studies of clients treated by behavior therapy.

E. G. P.

INTRODUCTION

IT is well known that those, who for psychological reasons fail to cope with their environment, rarely seek help from psychologists or psychiatrists in the first instance. Most often they initially turn to a general practitioner, a teacher, minister, friend, or relative (Gurin, Veroff and Feld, 1960). Each of these tends to interpret what he gleans from the help seeker in terms of his own personal experience or school of thought. Confronted with an adolescent drug abuser for instance, the physician may regard the problem primarily as a health hazard, the teacher may see it as a manifestation of social protest; to the minister it could suggest an existential crisis, while friends and relatives are apt to view it as an immature person's attempt to escape from a stressful life situation. Each of these formulations is likely to lead to different forms of advice or remedial action, varying from medication or increased permissiveness to pastoral counseling or eviction from home.

Occasionally, these methods do indeed have the desired effect. Only when they fail, do those who seek further help come to the attention of professionally trained change agents. At that point the layman's "personal experience" or "school of thought" is replaced by the professional's "clinical experience" and "theoretical orientation." Just as in the layman's case, these factors determine how the presenting problem will be formulated and treated. Again a wide range of remedial techniques may be suggested, each being endowed by its proponent with more or less "scientific" status. Here, too, the outcome is often favourable. When it is not, the next step is to try another method or to refer the problem to a colleague with a different orientation.

What is common to the layman and the professional person's handling of these cases is that each bases his method of intervention on hunches or hypotheses about the origin of the clinical problem. Whether he entertains these hypotheses explicitly, firmly or tentatively, with or without scientific pretension, is not crucial. What matters, in the present context, is that the outcome of each method, if favourable, is often taken as evidence that the causal hypothesis leading to treatment was, in fact, correct. Thus the drug addict who recovers after pastoral counseling is thereby regarded as having suffered from an existential crisis relieved by the counselor. Similarly, some would argue that the drug addict who does not respond to being placed in a more permissive environment was evidently not using drugs as a form of protest against authority. Circular reasoning of this sort is, or course, misleading, not because the presumed cause of a disorder is necessarily unrelated to interventions affecting it, but because in the absence of demonstrable cause-effect relations, the outcome of a remedial measure can never, logically, serve as confirmation of the theory from which the method of intervention was derived in the first place. In other words the demonstration that a particular way of dealing with drug abuse was effective, may be clinically encouraging, but permits of no inference about the etiology of such abuse.

Since we are ignorant about the causes of most behavioral deviations it is more expedient to evaluate remedial techniques purely in terms of their outcome and without reference to theories of psychopathology, whether or not these gave rise to the techniques in question. Some therapists would deplore this single-minded concern with outcome on the grounds that therapeutic processes, and not their consequences, are the thing to explore if existing techniques are to be improved or new ones found. But that point of view has not gone unchallenged. As Zubin (1965) has rightly observed: "There is a tendency current in some quarters to give up evaluating therapy and to resort instead to analyzing the process itself. This escape into process will never substitute for actual evaluation. No amount of investigation of 'the therapeutic process' is going to give us the answer as to whether psychotherapy was worthwhile in the first place" (p. 355).

The behavioral approach is one attempt to resolve this issue. Though learning theories provide the basis for most of its methods, their application does not rest on the assumption that all symptoms amenable to modification were solely acquired through learning. What is predicated is that most behavior disorders have components which were indeed acquired by some learning process and that alleviation of these components, by one of the conditioning therapies, could lead to social recovery in the sense that the disorder no longer impairs the individual's coping mechanism.

That aim differs from that of more traditional psychotherapies in that no attempt is made to influence the internal state of the individual directly, unless its manipulation leads to demonstrable behavioral consequences, as in the work of cognitive therapists like Cautela (1967), Ellis (1970), or Meichenbaum and Turk (1976). Also it is contrary to behavioral learning theories to assume that a person's maladaptive responses could be lastingly eliminated unless the pathogenic environment is also changed. Most behavior therapists accept responsibility for helping clients effect such environmental change should they be unable to do so on their own.

Ultimately, all forms of psychotherapy can be seen as attempts to help an individual deal more effectively with his environment. But nowhere is it done as explicitly as in the behavior therapies where the unit of behavior treated is often an operant, i.e. a response used by the client to "operate" on his environment. Moreover when this attempt at helping the client modify his own environment fails, the behavior therapist does not shrink from applying his techniques to that environment directly. That strategy has already led to useful innovations in the management of child-parent relations, child-teacher problems and in marital counseling (Becker, 1971; Patterson, 1971; O'Leary and Drabman, 1971; Stuart 1969).

It is sometimes argued that importance of the environment — particularly the client's early environment — as a determinant of later behavior was first emphasized by Freud and that he therefore taught a form of learning theory (Alexander, 1963). But that is misleading, because according to Freud, the child's environment determines not a specific learning process, but rather the nature and direction of his drives (Foppa, 1965). Again psychoanalytic theory has a great deal to say about the relationship of the individual to his environment but in the analytic treatment process therapists rarely attempt to modify specific aspects of the client's environment known to maintain his psychological impairment.

Behavior change agents, by contrast, see their main task as modifying those aspects of the change seeker's milieu which seem to maintain his maladaptive responses. To identify these features of the environment they conduct a behavioral analysis of the complaint or coping deficit. This is a procedure whereby the conditions controlling the occurrence and remission of symptoms are explored as fully as possible, not just verbally, but also by observation in different settings and, where possible, by deliberate variation of circumstances. A behavioral analysis, which should always precede treatment, is successful to the extent that it delineates at least the necessary if not the sufficient conditions maintaining the unwanted behavior. It could also be viewed as a technique whereby the client's verbal and nonverbal communications are rephrased in terms amenable to remedial action along behavioral lines.

The behavior modifier's insistence on dealing only with those factors which maintain behavior, but not with those presumed to cause it, is often seen as a form of oversimplification. That charge would be justified if it were the change agent's intent to eradicate all suboptimal characteristics of a client's conduct or to restructure his entire personality (if that were possible). But behavior change agents have no such lofty aims, not only because such a quest seems unrealistic at the present state of our knowledge, but also because there is reason to believe that successful modification of disturbing behavior frequently leads to a general amelioration of the individual's adjustment. No doubt this results from emergence of the unimpaired aspect of the client's behavioral repertoire previously masked by his more salient deficits. If a person is helped to overcome maladaptive responses, no matter how specific these may be, it seems self-evident that such a change must have salutary ramifications for the general adjustment of that person.

Focusing a treatment program on specific maladaptive behaviors, rather than on the general state or "total personality" of the change seeker, has other advantages. Above all it makes a behavioral analysis possible, and this enables a quantitative assessment of the presenting problems. Establishment of such a baseline helps one (a) to distinguish clearly between the variety of problems a client may have; (b) to decide which intervention is best suited to which problem; and (c) to measure the behavior change that may result from therapy. Of these procedures the last is by far the most important and the least recognized in other forms of psychotherapy, a fact which may account for the dearth of therapy outcome research prior to the 1960s. Since then a large number of individual case reports and group studies have appeared on the relative merits of many conditioning therapies. Thanks to these, it is now possible to predict, with increasing accuracy, which technique is likely to be most effective in counteracting a specific deviation. By the same logic, a pretreatment baseline of the behavior(s) to be modified, makes it possible to know when a particular treatment, which failed to produce the expected results, should have been altered or abandoned.

The question, "Who should receive behavior therapy?", has a long and somewhat confusing history in the clinical literature. In the late fifties and early sixties, when the first published case studies appeared, it was widely held that the conditioning therapies are effective only in monosymptomatic conditions such as certain phobias (Breger and McGaugh, 1965). This belief arose largely from the fact that early case studies of effective therapy — notably in Wolpe's (1958) first book *Psychotherapy by Reciprocal Inhibition* — were indeed largely conducted on patients with various forms of anxiety and circumscribed phobias. At that stage also, the term "behavior therapy" was all but synonymous with systematic desensitization, then by far the best known and researched conditioning procedure. To be sure, clinical work with operant techniques had started in the United States, even earlier, but was, prior to

1960, almost exclusively concerned with research on psychotic patients.

The last ten years have seen a major change in that trend. No longer are the conditioning techniques confined to two or three major methods, and documented evidence of their efficacy, in a wide variety of behavior disorders, is now legion. It ranges from the successful management of self-destructive and aggressive behavior in mentally defective and autistic children, as in the work of Bucher and his colleagues (Bucher and Lovaas 1968) to the treatment of complex anxiety states and compulsions by "flooding" or response prevention. (Wolpe, 1964, Marks, 1972).

Entire wards in mental hospitals are being managed by "token economy systems" (Di Scipio 1974), and the application of operant techniques, such as contingency management, is now widespread in schools and other educational establishments, including those concerned with teacher training.

But the principal development that shaped progress in behavior therapy since its inception, is a theoretical one. Whereas behavior therapy was, in its early stages inspired by stimulus-response theories, such as those of Pavlov, Thorndike and Hull, recent years have witnessed much greater recognition of cognitive variables as determinants of deviant behavior. As a result, an entirely new set of methods has evolved among which modeling and covert sensitization are perhaps the best known. In a way, cognitive elements were always involved in conditioning therapies (see for instance cognitive rehearsal as a component of systematic desensitization), but it took the theoretical and experimental contributions of authors like Homme (1965), Staats and Staats (1964), and Bandura (1971) to demonstrate that the manipulation of thoughts, images, fantasies, and perceptions can lead to behavioral consequences no less measurable than behavior more directly under external stimulus control.

Maladaptive behavior occurring in response to external cues is, of course, easier to control and modify, which accounts for the preference of most behavior therapists for treating phobias, sexual dysfunctions and some addictions, rather than mood disorders or psychotic reactions in which the eliciting stimuli are often very difficult, or impossible, to identify. Here again, recent work has shown that even these cases can occasionally benefit from conditioning therapy, though the improvements achieved may be more limited and less lasting than those of clients whose symptoms are situation-specific. (Lewinson, 1971; McLean, Ogston, and Grauer, 1973; Beck, 1970; and Lazarus, 1968).

In light of these considerations one is led to conclude that there is probably no category of behavior dysfunction for which all forms of behavior therapy are contraindicated. Certainly the present writer has seen very few clients whose condition was aggravated by techniques of behavior modification, judiciously selected and competently applied. Relapse, on the other hand, seems to be as frequent following behavior therapy, as it is after other forms of treatment, a fact documented by some of the case histories reported in this book. Since relapse rates are known to vary enormously depending on the nature of the problem, it often becomes a practical necessity to select those clients for whom behavior therapy is the treatment of choice. At present this would include all those behavior problems known to be primarily due to faulty learning and those which are elicitable through manipulation of specific stimuli. Phobic reactions, social withdrawal, bedwetting, many anxiety states leading to maladaptive avoidance behavior, certain epilepsies, some addictions, and many learning problems in children are cases in point. Neurotic and endogenous depressions, as well as most other affective disorders of long standing, psychotic symptoms and behavioral deficits due to brain damage are much more difficult to treat by conditioning methods. The same is true of those disorders in which the deviant behavior is itself powerfully reinforcing as in drug addiction, alcoholism, sexual aberrations, and criminality. That is not to say that applicants for behavior change from these "poor prognosis groups" should be rejected, but it does mean that for clients in this category the goals of therapy must be kept at a more modest level. Also the greater demands these clients make on the staff and resources of a clinic should be clearly recognized from the start.

Once the extent of a behavioral impairment is known, some other questions need to be clarified before treatment can begin. Apart from eliminating physical illness (or making arrangements for its treatment elsewhere) it is useful to obtain certain kinds of information from the client. Essentially this is of three kinds:

1. *Historical information as found in traditional psychiatric anamneses and more behaviorally oriented questionnaires, such as that developed by Kanfer and Saslow (1969).* We have also found personal history forms, which the patient completes in his own time, helpful in this context.
2. *Information relating to diagnosis and prognosis.* This is of particular significance in case selection, though the diagnostic selection criteria should be based on behavioral findings, which may or may not jibe with nosological criteria commonly applied in selecting patients for other forms of therapy. So far only a few tests helpful in prognosis have been developed, but there are some, such as a fourteen-item inventory found to predict the outcome of desensitization therapy (Gelder et al, 1967).
3. *Information to be used in the modification process, such as an inventory of the client's likes and dislikes as reflected in the Fear Survey Schedule (Geer, 1965), the Reward Schedule (Cautela and Kastenbaum, 1967), or similar pencil and paper tests.*

Regrettably, most of the instruments currently available for obtaining information, particularly in the second category, are poorly suited to the needs of behavior therapists. The reason is obvious; the vast majority of existing techniques for diagnostic and prognostic assessment of clients were derived from dynamic theories of psychopathology for the purpose of assigning conventional labels of psychiatric nosology. What is presently lacking are instruments relating standardized behavior samples

(a) to specific manifestations of maladjustment and
(b) to variables likely to affect these manifestations, i.e. aspects of the client's behavioral repertoire amenable to change.

If, for instance, the presenting symptom is that of bedwetting, generally viewed by behavior therapists as a deficit in the acquisition of appropriate conditioned muscular responses, it would be more useful to obtain a conditioning profile of that child and to discover whether he responds better to classical or operant conditioning techniques, than to infer that he is overly dependent on his mother and potentially neurotic. Though scarce at present, behavior-specific assessment techniques are now being developed and should greatly increase the efficiency of pretreatment evaluations.

Nor should objective assessments cease at that stage. The number of reassessments to be done will depend on the nature of the problem, but always the pretreatment baseline provides the major point of reference. Results of these tests should be graphically recorded, thus providing progress charts for easy reference. In selected cases, as in the treatment of obesity, for example, prominent display of weight charts in the clients' living quarters may enhance their motivation.

Little has yet been said in the clinical literature about termination criteria. Though most therapists would claim that they terminate treatment when the symptom has been alleviated or eliminated, it is unlikely that another therapist, dealing with the same patient, would terminate treatment at precisely the same time. It is also evident that the point of termination is as often decided by the client as by the therapist. This is due to a variety of reasons, ranging from personal convenience to insolvency. If to this one adds the well-known fact that some clients, by virtue of likeability or other reinforcing influence they exert on the therapist, are likely to be retained in therapy longer, very little scope for objective planning of treatment termination is left to the change agent.

Perhaps all that need be said, in principle, is that, wherever possible, behavior therapeutic interventions should never end abruptly from one day to the next. Before termination of therapy the patient should always be given a chance to perform outside the therapeutic situation those behavioral sequences he could not master before treatment. Generally, it is during that final phase of therapy that others in the client's environment

take on some of the functions hitherto discharged by the therapist. Often the patient quite spontaneously casts certain
members of his family in the therapist's role; at other times
relatives make that decision. If this does not happen, the therapist's help may be needed to select and, if necessary, to instruct
the most suitable "ally in reinforcement." In the case of
children, and with hospitalized clients, the change agent typically works closely with parents, teachers, or nursing staff from
the very beginning, but at no time is this teamwork more crucial than at the point where the client returns to the setting in
which his symptoms first appeared. Presumably he is now
better equipped to deal with that environment, but in the transition period, there may well be occasional set-backs that are
more easily overcome in the presence of a friend or relative
"who knows what to do."

Even at that point, the therapist's work is still incomplete.
The all important follow-up remains to be done. For some
patients this takes the form of "booster" sessions in which a
particular intervention is repeated at decreasing frequency,
sometimes for many months, before it is faded out. In other
cases the follow-up serves to "troubleshoot" minor difficulties
encountered by the client, before these assume unmanageable
proportions. In all cases, the follow-up provides the therapist
with valuable feedback as to the long-term efficacy of his efforts. Only in this way can he discover where he went wrong
and how he might modify his procedure in future treatment of
similar cases. Last but not least, the change agent derives from
the follow-up, at least intermittent, reinforcement for what he
has done. Perhaps because it is intermittent, it preserves the
change agent's clinical zeal from the untimely extinction it may
otherwise undergo.

In what is to follow, the general guidelines for applied behavior therapy presented in this introductory chapter will be
illustrated by case material. Throughout, the emphasis will be
on how information obtained, from or about a client, was used
to arrive at a treatment programme, how the programme was
carried out and what considerations most influenced the
decision-making process. Three major problem areas are

covered: specific fears, physical expressions of social withdrawal, and socially disapproved behavior. Several interventions appropriate to each of these categories of impairment are discussed.

To permit long-term, follow-up data to be included, those cases were selected whose treatment was completed at least five years ago. For some the follow-up period was close to ten years. This goes back to a time when the Douglas Hospital Behavior Therapy Unit was first started, when one had little experience and less equipment. Also many methods now available were then unknown. Were the same clients to be treated today much would be done differently. Even so, old cases were selected because the short-term effect of behavior therapy has been well documented in many books and journals, whereas follow-up data for longer than two years are still very rare. To compensate the reader for the historical perspective he is asked to adopt, the original documentation at the end of each chapter is supplemented by suggested readings from the contemporary literature.

Each chapter heading refers to a specific behavior problem and to the main technique employed to deal with it. This was done for convenience only. In practice most cases turn out to have a multiplicity of symptoms and consequently call for a variety of counteracting measures. Hence it is by no means always clear which of the methods used was indeed the "major intervention." The phrase merely refers to what, in the author's view, was the treatment of choice for the major symptom causing the client to seek help. Additional methods used are listed as such at the beginning of each chapter. Except where otherwise stated all patients were hospitalized and under regular medical care at the time of receiving behavior therapy.

A word of explanation about some of the other subheadings adopted in the case presentations may be helpful.

FAMILY BACKGROUND. Only the bare essentials are included, unless this aspect of the case was evidently relevant to the presenting behavior problem.

PERSONAL HISTORY. Here again, no attempt was made to present the entire history as it might appear in a psychiatric anamnesis. Only major events in the client's personal growth and development are recorded, with special reference to those seemingly related to the present problem.

HISTORY OF PRESENT PROBLEMS. Wherever available, this is given in considerable detail. It is generally based on the patient's own account or on that of close relatives.

BEHAVIOR ANALYSIS. A clear distinction is made between information obtained from interviews, field observations, or tests. The last two generally provide data for the baseline determinations. No attempt was made to reproduce the raw data, but summary statements of test scores are provided for most cases.

TREATMENT GOALS. These are listed to enable the reader to judge for himself in which cases, and to what extent, the methods used achieved their aim.

TREATMENTS. Each intervention used is described in sufficient detail to give the nonspecialized reader at least a general idea of what was done. Suggestions for further readings are listed at the end of each chapter.

TREATMENT EVALUATION. Wherever possible the effect of treatments is evaluated in terms of behavior change relative to the baseline. Decisions to continue, change, or terminate therapy are based on this assessment.

DECISION TO TERMINATE. Specific reasons leading to that decision are reviewed for every case. As will be seen, the point of termination was not always determined by the change agent. Even when it was, the decision to terminate was sometimes taken in error.

FOLLOW-UP. Before this book went to press each of the eight clients reported on was asked to return for a structured interview. This was arranged and conducted by one of two assistants* who had never before met these clients. The questionnaires, a copy of which is reproduced in the Appendix, were filled out by the interviewers and reflect as closely as possible the verbatim responses given by the clients. Only after completion of these interviews was each client seen by the author whose impressions are recorded to supplement the questionnaire data. In addition, various other techniques of

---

*Thanks are due to Sherry Pitcher and George Garneau for their persistence and sensitivity in gathering these data.

gathering post-treatment information from clients are described. The findings illustrate the importance of arranging the client's "reinforcement destiny" before treatment is terminated.

RETROSPECTIVE APPRAISAL. Hindsight may be a poor prophet, but it is a good teacher. On termination of treatment it is often easier to see where mistakes were made and how difficult it is to identify the "active ingredients" of an intervention supposedly associated with its outcome.

Where appropriate, a section headed "Comment" is inserted to clarify a point or to draw the readers attention to an unusual aspect of procedural or methodological significance. For obvious reasons many descriptive details about clients were disguised to protect their anonymity. Even so, the major course of events, over time, was faithfully recorded as it occurred. Particular care was taken to convey the follow-up information as closely as possible to the way in which it was received, and with a minimum of editorial distortion.

The term "patient," to describe a recipient of behavior therapy, was avoided throughout this book wherever possible. There are several reasons for this: The word derives from a "medical model" conceptually at variance with some basic tenets of behavior modification; the derivation of the term "patient" (from Old French "to suffer") suggests a degree of passive endurance quite inconsistent with the behavior modifier's demands upon the persons he treats; perhaps the most important consideration of all is that the new coinage "change agent," instead of therapist, and "behavior modification," instead of treatment, has found acceptance in recent years. It seems incongruous that "change agents" should modify the behavior of "patients." If the words "therapist" and "treatment" have yielded to behavioral reinterpretation, why not the term "patient?" Admittedly, this author did not succeed in finding a single acceptable alternative. For this reason he has taken refuge in diversity and used a variety of synonyms for "patient," depending on the context.

REFERENCES

Alexander, F.: The dynamics of psychotherapy in the light of learning theory.

Am J Psychiatry, 120:440-448, 1963.

Bandura, A.: Self-reinforcement processes. In R. Glaser (Ed.): *The Nature of Reinforcement.* New York, Acad Pr, 1971.

Beck, A. T.: Cognitive therapy, nature and relation to behavior therapy. *Behav Ther, 1*:184-200, 1970.

Becker, W. C.: *Parents are Teachers.* Champaign, Res Press, 1971.

Breger, L., and McGaugh, J. L.: Critique and reformulation of learning theory approaches to psychotherapy and neurosis. *Psychological Bulletin, 63*:338-358, 1965.

Bucher, B., and Lovaas, O. I.: Use of aversive stimulation in behavior modification. In· M. R. Jones (Ed.): *Miami Symposium on the Prediction of Behavior.* 1967. Aversive stimulation. Miami, U of Miami Pr, 1968.

Cautela, J. R.: Covert Sensitization. *Psychol Rep, 20*:459-468, 1967.

Cautela, J. R., and Kastenbaum, R. A.: A reinforcement survey schedule for use in therapy, training, and research. *Psychol Rep, 20*:1115-1130, 1967.

DiScipio, W. J.: The Behavioral Treatment of Psychiatric Illness. New York, *Behavioral Publications*, pp. 240, 1974.

Ellis, A.: *Reason and Emotion in Psychotherapy.* New York, Lyle Stuart, 1970.

Foppa, K.: *Lernen, Gedaechtnis, Verhalten.* Berlin, Kiepenheuer and Witsch, p. 313, 1965.

Geer, J. H.: The development of a scale to measure fear. *Behav Res Ther, 3*:45-53, 1965.

Gelder, M. G., Marks, I. M., and Wolff, H. H.: Desensitization and psychotherapy in the treatment of phobic states. A controlled inquiry. *Br J Psychiatry, 113*:55-73, 1967.

Gurin, G., Veroff, J., and Feld, S.: *Americans View Their Mental Health: A Nationwide Survey.* New York, Basic, 1960.

Homme, L. E.: Perspectives in psychology XXIV. Control of coverants, operants of the mind. *Psychol Rec, 15*:501-511, 1965.

Kanfer, F. H., and Saslow, G.: Behavioral diagnosis. From C. M. Franks (Ed.): *Behavior Therapy: Appraisal and Status.* New York, McGraw, 1969.

Lazarus, A.: Learning theory and the treatment of depression. *Behav Res Ther, 6*:83-89, 1968.

Lewinsohn, P. M.: A behavioral approach to depression. In R. M. Freidman, and M. M. Katz (Eds.): *The·Psychology of Depression: Contemporary Theory and Research.* New York, Halstead, 1971.

Marks, I. M.: Perspective on flooding. *Seminars in Psychiatry, 4*:129-138, May 1972.

McLean, P. D., Ogston, K., and Grauer, L.: A behavioral approach to depression. *Journal of Behavioral Therapy and Experimental Psychiatry, 4*:323-330, 1973.

Meichenbaum, D., and Turk, D.: The cognitive-behavioral management of anxiety, anger, and pain. From P. O. Davidson (Ed.): *The Behavioral*

Management of Anxiety, Depression and Pain. New York, Brunner/Mazel, 1976.

O'Leary, D., and Drabman, R.: Token reinforcement in the classroom: a review. *Psychological Bulletin, 75*:379-398, 1971.

Patterson, G. R.: Behavioral intervention procedures in the classroom and in the home. In A. E. Bergin, and S. L. Garfield (Eds.): *Handbook of Psychotherapy and Behavior Change: An Empirical Analysis.* New York, Wiley, 751-775, 1971.

Staats, A. W., and Staats, C. K.: *Complex Human Behavior.* New York, R & W, 1964.

Stuart, R. B.: Operant interpersonal treatment for marital discord. *J Consult Clin Psychol, 6*:675-682, 1969.

Wolpe, J.: Psychotherapy by reciprocal inhibition. Stanford, Stanford U Pr, 1958.

Wolpe, J.: Behavior therapy in complex neurotic states. *Br J Psychiatry, 110*:28-34, 1964.

Zubin, J., and Burdock, E. I.: The revolution in psychopathology and its implications for public health. *Acta Psychiatrica Scand, 4*:348-359, 1965.

CONTENTS

BEHAVIOR THERAPY
IN CLINICAL PRACTICE

Illustrative Case Material

PART ONE: SPECIFIC FEARS

CHAPTER 1

RELAXATION AND MODIFIED SYSTEMATIC DESENSITIZATION

BEHAVIOR PROBLEM: *Fear of leaving place of residence*
PSYCHIATRIC DIAGNOSIS: *Character Neurosis (agoraphobia)*
MAJOR INTERVENTION: *Relaxation and systematic desensitization (modified)*
ADDITIONAL METHODS USED: *"In vivo" desensitization and contingency management*

General appearance, main complaint, and circumstances at intake:

Mrs. M. had been housebound for six years before she was referred for treatment at the age of forty-two. She had a tense, emaciated appearance, spoke abruptly, and moved clumsily. She wore no make-up and seemed to be generally untidy about her person.

Her attitude was one of marked hostility and sarcasm. At first she refused treatment, claiming that she could deal with her problems alone. Most of her difficulties she ascribed to mismanagement by various mental health professionals consulted in the past. At the same time she expressed surprise that anyone should want to bother with her, since she regarded her condition as hopeless. The contradictory nature of her self-report seemed to evade her.

She expressed particular distaste for men, and at first refused admission to the Behavior Therapy Unit even when she was offered a female therapist. At one time she had been treated privately in her own home, which she shared with her sister. When the latter decided to get married, Mrs. M. could no longer manage on her own and, after much persuasion, entered a private nursing home. She could not be maintained there any longer because of her phobic symptoms and her belligerent attitude towards the staff. She was told that behavior therapy was available to her, but that she would not be admitted against her will. Twenty-four hours later she reluctantly asked to be transferred to the Behavior Therapy Unit.

FAMILY BACKGROUND:

The client is the oldest daughter by her father's first marriage. When the client was three years old, her mother died of heart disease soon after the birth of a second daughter. Her father then remarried and there were four children, all boys, by that union. The client expressed little affection for her stepmother and nothing but contempt for her father, whom she described as a "lascivious pervert" who made sexual advances to youngsters of both sexes. She also claimed that he had interfered sexually with her and vividly recalls a similar episode involving her younger sister. The father died of a kidney ailment at the age of sixty-eight.

PERSONAL HISTORY:

Mrs. M.'s early development was uneventful apart from one brief hospitalisation for an appendectomy. When she was five or six-years-old her father became sexually aroused in her presence and prevailed upon her to lie in bed with him. This she recalls with tremendous abhorrence.

At the age of seven, she was placed in a day-care centre while her stepmother went to work in a laundry. She did this to supplement the family income, because her husband, a railroad worker, drank heavily.

Although Mrs. M. did very well in school at all times, she was sent to work at the age of fifteen and thus could not finish high school. She hated her father for not allowing her to complete her education.

At eighteen she was married to a man she had known for only two months. He left her within a year to live with another woman. To earn a living, she took a job as a salesgirl and attended evening classes to obtain her high school diploma. Subsequently she obtained employment as a waitress and later as a cashier in the same establishment. She had few friends and apart from her younger sister, with whom she set up house, her social contacts were sparse. She did most of the cleaning and housekeeping; her sister did all of the shopping.

HISTORY OF PRESENT PROBLEM:

The onset of Mrs. M.'s difficulty is hard to establish. She never felt comfortable in male company and hastily entered marriage only because she found life at home intolerable. Her husband's desertion came as a relief to her, and at no time did she experience satisfactory sexual relations with him, or anyone else. She was not surprised at his leaving her since she always regarded herself as physically unattractive. "I never understood why he wanted to marry me in the first place," she commented.

Nor did she have any close relationships with women. For convenience she kept on friendly terms with a number of girls at work with whom she occasionally went to a movie or on a picnic, but none of these acquaintances were important to her. At the age of twenty-nine she recalls having had a brief infatuation for a man in his fifties, but when it turned out that he had a wife that he had not told her about, she refused to see him again. After that time she led an increasingly solitary life. She gave up her job when her father died and left her some money, and for the last six years never left the house except when absolutely necessary, and then only in the company of her sister. Such friends as she had visited her less and less often because of Mrs. M.'s unwillingness to join in their activities and also because of her mounting hostility. When the sister decided to get married, Mrs. M. was no longer able to cope. She agreed to enter a nursing home but had to be taken there by ambulance, as she was too fearful to leave home on her own.

COMMENT:

Judged by the anamnesis, the roots of Mrs. M.'s severe agoraphobic symptoms reside in her early family relationships. She spoke of these only with the utmost difficulty, and would not verbalise any details though she claimed to remember each sexual adventure with her father "as if it were yesterday." Her conversation on this topic mainly consisted of incomplete sentences followed by embarrassed giggles, quite out of keeping with her usually reserved and truculent manner.

The onset of her condition was insidious, and she became incapacitated only because of an unavoidable change in her life situation. Had her sister not been married at this time, the client might well have managed to live with her symptoms until some other event in her environment had interfered with her dependency. At the beginning of treatment in the Behavior Therapy Unit she had still not decided whether to put up with her symptoms or to have them alleviated. Her reluctance to be admitted was probably due to this conflict.

BEHAVIOR ANALYSIS: *Interview.*

An interview conducted with the client's sister bore out much of what Mrs. M. had said. The sister agreed that her father had been very promiscuous, but denied that she too had been the object of his sexual advances, as Mrs. M. had alleged. She described her sister as "very intelligent, but full of crazy ideas." She also revealed that the funds left to her by her father would only suffice to keep her sister for another year, and she did not see how Mrs. M. would manage after that, unless she changed her ideas and behavior. As far as she could tell, her sister would have to live on public welfare, probably in some boarding home. She spoke of her with kindness, but made it very clear that she could henceforth not be counted upon to care for Mrs. M., nor to participate in her rehabilitation.

Asked about her sister's activities in the home, it became apparent that she was quite efficient as a housekeeper, but terrified of venturing outside the home. She would potter about in the garden, but only when someone she knew was present. The last time Mrs. M. had been on the street with her sister — over two years ago — was to have dental treatment and to buy some clothes. While in the dentist's office, and later in the store, she was relatively calm, but when waiting for the bus to go home, the client began to shake violently all over, sweated profusely, and then rushed into the nearest building. From there the sister brought her home by taxi. The client's contact with reality was apparently unimpaired. However, most of her conversation was said to be gloomy, laconic, and hostile.

BEHAVIOR ANALYSIS: *Observations.*

The client first came to the hospital in midwinter. Observations were hampered during the first week of her stay because of extremely cold weather conditions. Even so, it was possible to establish that she could reach the hospital gates (about a five minute walk from the unit) on her own, but she would not leave the hospital grounds, even when accompanied. She felt more comfortable in company of a nurse rather than that of a male staff member, but no one could induce her to venture beyond the hospital gates.

During the early part of her stay on the ward, no hostility was noted toward staff or fellow patients. This was in striking contrast to her preadmission behavior, when she vilified most professionals who had tried to help her and went so far as to blame her illness on the medical mismanagement of her case.

She was found to be rather careless about her personal appearance, walked around in a dressing gown all day, but kept her room clean and tidy. She also volunteered to help others on the ward who could not care for themselves. Most of the time, however, she kept to herself reading or watching television.

BEHAVIOR ANALYSIS: *Tests.*

Mrs. M. had been given a full battery of psychological tests prior to admission. This included the WAIS and some personality questionnaires. Later the Fear Survey Schedule and Willoughby Anxiety Questionnaire were administered and also some electrodermal measures of arousal level were obtained.

Her full scale IQ was 118 and showed very little sub-test

scatter. Her personality profile was that of an introverted person with some hysterical features. As often happens, there were very few test indications of her behavioral impairment.

On the Fear Survey Schedule (Lang and Lazovik, 1963) she checked items such as "strange and high places," "large open spaces," "journeys" and "crowds" as being highly fear-provoking. Two items she added to the list of major fears were "the future" and "treatment." On the Willoughby (1934) Questionnaire she indicated very high anxiety.

Her verbal report was borne out by measures taken of her electrodermal response to certain imagined situations such as "being in a crowded bus" or "going out alone." By comparison to her GSR activity while contemplating a neutral, relaxing scene, her arousal level (increased skin conductance) was very noticeable when fear-provoking items were suggested. These fluctuations in autonomic response were later used to arrive at the order of·items in her desensitization hierarchy.

TREATMENT GOALS:

(1) The client should be helped to overcome those fears which currently restrict her mobility.
(2) Her social and occupational rehabilitation should be facilitated.

THERAPEUTIC STRATEGY:

The range of fears associated with Mrs. M.'s inability to move about freely outside her own familiar surroundings was very wide indeed. Among others, it involved interpersonal fears, crowds, high places, and physical displacement. Her interpersonal fears, in particular, were so intense that she could not initially communicate them to the therapist with any degree of clarity. Therefore, implosive therapy, which depends upon the therapist's ability to reactivate for the client images of former traumatic situations, would not have been feasible in this case.

Again, the fears were too diffuse to extinguish the avoidance responses they produced by flooding or response prevention.

Also radical approaches of this sort, in an already reluctant client, might well have led to complete refusal of further treatment.

By process of elimination, the method of systematic desensitization was selected as the most promising first step. Once she became mobilised again, her social skills could be improved by contingently rewarding her attempts to reach out, make, and maintain social contacts, while any attempt at social withdrawal would meet with loss of privileges. A reward schedule she had been asked to complete earlier had shown that she was fond of fine foods, music, and clothes. These were some of the items to be made available to her in the second part of her program, contingent upon the desired behavior change. Finally, vocational testing and services of the hospital's placement officer were to be brought to bear in the interest of the client's occupational rehabilitation.

TREATMENT METHOD: *Desensitization* in vivo.

Initially an attempt was made to give relaxation training in the manner of Jacobson (1938) as a preliminary to the construction of desensitization hierarchies (Wolpe, 1958). In Mrs. M.'s case, this attempt had to be abandoned after five sessions, because there was no sign of progress.

Clients do, of course, vary widely in their capacity to learn relaxation. Some are habitually so tense that such relaxation as they can achieve does not provide sufficient feedback for them to differentiate tension from relaxation in a particular muscle group. Others have no trouble learning that discrimination, but are afraid to relax. Both groups can generally acquire the relaxation response eventually, even though a much longer training period, or even the use of cortically depressant drugs such as Brietal® or Diazepam®, may be required (Pecknold et al., 1972, and Brady, 1967).

For Mrs. M., the request that she enter the relaxation room seemed to be a signal for increased bodily tension. She lay on the bed in a rigid manner, and though she seemed to concentrate on what was being said to her, it was evident from her facies and bodily posture that no relaxation was taking place. Her verbal report confirmed this impression. In subsequent sessions, an easy chair was used instead of the bed, and an older, female therapist was substituted for the original, younger one. It made no difference. Each session left her in a more rigid state than she had been in before entering the relaxation room. After three attempts by one therapist and two by another, the use of medication was suggested. This she flatly refused, especially when she learned that the drug would be given by injection. Even the offer to administer the drug by mouth met with total rejection.

For these reasons it was decided to proceed with a program of desensitization *in vivo*. This was considered second best because the behavioral analysis had already indicated that the greatest fear maintaining Mrs. M.'s agoraphobia derived from interpersonal situations, which are notoriously difficult to treat *in vivo* unless preceded by some form of cognitive rehearsal, as in reciprocal inhibition therapy.

Initially *in vivo* desensitization was presented to Mrs. M. as an extension of the observation procedure with which she was already familiar. Each day she was to distance herself from the ward as far as she could comfortably tolerate. The degree of comfort was to be subjectively assessed by her on a ten-point, self-rating scale. A rating of zero signified complete absence of discomfort or nervous tension, whereas a rating of ten represented extreme discomfort or the wish to escape from that situation. At first she was taken out alone by a staff member of her choice, who was instructed to bring her back as soon as she reported a discomfort rating above five. After awhile, she joined a group of other clients being taken out for the same purpose. Once she had reached a certain location repeatedly, but could not get beyond it, a slightly more distant aim was set for her. On reaching it, she was rewarded, generally by some happening that could not have occurred had she not travelled the extra distance. If, for instance, she had managed to reach a point which was six bus stops from the hospital, it was suggested she try one eight stops away, where there was a clothing store she used to frequent. On reaching that point, she could purchase an article of her choice.

At first, her progress was very satisfactory. After twenty outings over a period of five weeks, she was able to travel in company, about four miles toward the center of town. But on her own she went only as far as the nearest corner store, less than two blocks from the hospital. These gains were consolidated and slightly extended in the next thirty-five sessions, after which she made no further progress. By this time she could go to the centre of town on foot or by bus, enter stores, use escalators as well as elevators and tolerate crowded areas. All of this, however, she would do only when accompanied. It was striking that she gained little personal satisfaction from these accomplishments. Unlike many agoraphobic patients who experience great exultation every time they recapture a part of their previous behavioral repertoire, Mrs. M. greeted these occasions with indifference. She showed no initiative as far as going out alone was concerned. When urged to go out, she would rarely get further than three blocks from the hospital, complaining that she felt terrified when out on her own.

TREATMENT METHOD: *Reciprocal Inhibition.*

In order to help her to progress beyond the plateau she had reached, relaxation training — with a view to later desensitization — was once again attempted. Another female therapist undertook the treatment, and this time felt that the client made sufficient progress to proceed with desensitization in fantasy.

A hierarchy was constructed in which the first item was "going half way to the gate" and the most difficult image was "getting onto the subway." Despite the fact that she had already been to the centre of town, in company of others many times, she could not get beyond the second item of the hierarchy in the first two sessions, without signalling anxiety. In the third session she passed six of the thirteen steps in the hierarchy; in the fourth session ten items; in the fifth, eleven; and in the sixth session all of the items were negotiated.

Neither the therapist nor the client was convinced that desensitization had, in fact, taken place. Instead, the client, who knew what was expected of her, tried to cooperate by progressively omitting signals of anxiety as the sessions progressed. This was fairly evident from inspection of the desensitization chart, as it is uncommon for a client who cannot get beyond the second item on two successive occasions, to master thirteen items within the next four sessions.

Not only did the client admit that her response to the hierarchy items had not been significantly affected by the desensitization procedure, but behavioral tests of her mobility outside the hospital also showed no change. Clearly, some roadblock had been reached, beyond which she could not progress.

Other hierarchies were tried, until finally, six months after her admission, she volunteered the information that nothing would resolve her fears until she could be relieved of some dreadful fantasies, too horrendous to be imparted to anyone.

Much to her surprise, she was not urged to reveal these upsetting thoughts, but simply to arrange them, hierarchically, in the order from the least to the most distressing, and to identify each fantasy by a code-word meaningful to her, but not to anyone else. This she did, and desensitization henceforth, took the form of the therapist saying the code word and the client signalling if the code word reduced her level of relaxation in any way.

At first, even the code words produced the same embarrassed giggle, already noted during the intake interview. This response diminished over time and disappeared after the tenth session. After twenty-five desensitization sessions, held in the course of six weeks, the client managed to tolerate every item for periods of fifteen to twenty seconds. Ten overlearning sessions were held in the next two weeks, by which time every item was tolerated for twenty-five seconds or more.

For the first time since her admission, Mrs. M. showed interest in seeking a job near the hospital, and her self-initiated outings increased in frequency and distance covered. On occasion, when she had a definite reason for doing so, she could go to town alone, though she preferred to go in company. Change agents were careful never to take any new accomplishments for granted. Thus every indication that she had gone a little further afield, used a different form of public transport, or entered into some form of personal interaction, at once met with profuse social reinforcement.

DECISION TO TERMINATE TREATMENT:

The desensitization hierarchy having been completed, the programme next called for aid in her social and occupational rehabilitation

Vocational testing was in fact carried out, but before its results could be acted upon, the client had found part-time employment on her own. She wanted to work for a nearby car dealer who needed help in his office. Plans to involve Mrs. M. in behavior rehearsal, preliminary to her discharge, were therefore abandoned. She continued to live in the hospital while going to work, spending her spare time looking for a place to live. On finding suitable quarters near her place of work, she left the hospital.

FINAL EVALUATION:

Within the first four months of her stay in the Behavior Therapy Unit, the initial Willoughby Anxiety Questionnaire score of seventy-two had dropped to forty-three. It will be recalled that that was the point at which desensitization *in vivo*, had been completed. Similarly her Fear Survey Schedule, of which twelve items were initially rated as being "very much" anxiety provoking, now showed only seven such items. The total score on that schedule dropped from 148 to 88 in the first four months of treatment. Unfortunately, these tests were not repeated at the time of discharge.

She now spent all day off the ward, working either outside the hospital or helping in the hospital pharmacy. She socialized readily with staff and other clients she knew well. Her attitude to strangers remained cautious, particularly with men. She was not on medication of any sort, and she appeared cheerful and reasonably relaxed.

FOLLOW-UP:

In the five years since leaving hospital, Mrs. M. has continued living on her own and earning her keep. For the last two years she has been working as a saleslady in a clothing store. She found this position on her own, and her employer is highly satisfied with her services. Her spare-time activities consist mainly of reading, knitting, watching TV, and taking walks in a nearby park. Her social activities are few, but she occasionally plays Bingo in the local church and visits her relatives on weekends.

RETROSPECTIVE APPRAISAL:

This was a difficult client to treat. Not only did she have a long history of impairment, but initially she was quite resistant to accepting any kind of treatment. In spite of these obstacles, she made satisfactory progress once her basic anxieties, which in this case stemmed from certain childhood memories, were identified and desensitized.

The manner in which this was done constitutes a significant departure from standard desensitization procedure. The use of coded hierarchy items commends itself for use in similar cases where clients do not wish to disclose details of their bothersome thoughts or fantasies.

As frequently noted in the follow-up of agoraphobic clients, Mrs. M. has not totally mastered the fears which caused her to remain housebound for so long. She still lives and works near the hospital and admits that this is for reasons of security "should she relapse." But she is able to live on her own, to fend for herself and to get satisfaction from doing so. Barring further social rebuffs or other stresses to which she is particularly susceptible, her chances of continued improvement are likely to increase as she moves farther afield without experiencing undue distress.

TOTAL TIME IN BEHAVIOR THERAPY: *Fourteen months.*

REFERENCES

Brady, J. P.: Comments on methohexitone — aided systematic desensitization. *Behav Res and Ther*, 5:259-260, 1967.

Jacobson, E.: *Progressive Relaxation*. Chicago, U of Chicago Pr, 1938.

Lang, P. J., and Lazovik, A. D.: Experimental desensitization of a phobia. *Journal of Abnormal and Social Psychology*, 66:519-525, 1963.

Munjack, D. J.: Overcoming obstacles to desensitization using *in vivo* stimuli and brevital. *Behav Ther*, 6:543-546, 1975.

Pecknold, J. C., Raeburn, J., and Poser, E. G.: Intravenous diazepam for facilitating relaxation for desensitization. *Journal of Behavior Therapy and Experimental Psychiatry*, 3:39-41, 1972.

Russell, R. K., and Matthews, C. O.: Cue-controlled relaxation in vivo desensitization of a snake phobia. *Journal of Behavior Therapy and Experimental Psychiatry*, 6:49-52, 1975.

Willoughby, R. R.: Norms for the Clark-Thurston inventory. *Journal of Social Psychology*, 5:91, 1934.

Wolpe, J.: *Psychotherapy by Reciprocal Inhibition*. Stanford, Stanford U Pr, 1959.

Supplementary Readings

Rostow, C. D., and Smith, C. E.: Effects of contingency management of chronic patients on ward control and behavioral adjustment. *Journal of Behavioral Therapy and Experimental Psychiatry*, 6:1-4, 1975.

Silverstone, T. F.: The use of drugs in behavior therapy. *Behav Ther*, 1:485-497, 1970.

Weathers, L., and Liberman, R. P.: The family contracting exercise. *Journal of Behavior Therapy and Experimental Psychiatry*, 6:208-214, 1975.

CHAPTER 2

FLOODING IN VIVO

BEHAVIORAL PROBLEM: *Maladaptive avoidance responses and excessive handwashing*
PSYCHIATRIC DIAGNOSIS: *Obsessive compulsive neurosis*
MAJOR INTERVENTION: *Flooding (response prevention)*
ADDITIONAL METHODS USED: *Implosive therapy, assertive training, thought stoppage*

General appearance, main complaint and circumstances at intake:

This forty-three-year-old lady was referred for behavior therapy six years ago. One year earlier she had been admitted to another hospital where she received a variety of treatments, including ECT, antidepressant medication, and some conditioning therapy. She was now asking for help on the grounds that her constant preoccupation with germs and illness, but particularly with the disease carrying properties of raw meat, had become so intrusive that she could no longer fulfill her duties as mother and housewife.

Her appearance was rather plain. She was somewhat overweight for her height, soft spoken and neatly, but not meticulously, dressed. At the first interview, to which she came with her husband, she seemed quite depressed but was able to give a clear account of her history. She and her husband felt that she could no longer function in the home, and they were visibly relieved when hospitalisation was suggested.

FAMILY BACKGROUND:

Mrs. R. is the youngest of four children. The sibling closest to her is ten years older. She has always been fond of this sister and still sees her regularly. She describes her seventy-five-year-old mother as being a very friendly, good natured woman on whom she relies a great deal for reassurance.

Mrs. R.'s father died of cancer nine years ago. She says he was a good father to her but rather distant. He worked as a garage mechanic. All siblings are married and in good health. The only family member she recalls as having had some psychiatric illness was a paternal uncle who died in a mental hospital. Apparently he was a war casualty said to have suffered from "shell shock."

PERSONAL HISTORY:

Mrs. R. describes herself as having been overly dependent, apprehensive, nervous, and high-strung for as long as she can remember. Though she had no serious illness in infancy or childhood she frequently stayed away from school because of minor respiratory infections. She completed ninth grade and then took a part-time job as a sales girl in a grocery store.

She was married eighteen years ago to a man three years older than herself. He is a withdrawn, passive person who works as a shipping clerk and feels resentful about his life situation.

At first he apparently had considerable understanding for his wife's difficulties, but more recently he has become impatient with her inability "to pull herself together." Both partners describe their marriage as having been satisfactory until about four years ago when the youngest of their three children was five years old. Since that time Mr. R. claims to have lost interest in his wife sexually.

Until two years ago they lived in an annex to a house occupied by Mrs. R.'s parents, but now they have a duplex in a new housing development.

HISTORY OF PRESENT PROBLEM:

As far as she can recall Mrs. R. felt reasonably well until about thirteen years ago. Even before that time she was often anxious and insecure when put into positions of responsibility. The onset of her compulsive behaviour she relates to the birth of her second child, a boy now twelve-and-a-half-years-old. He was born prematurely by Caesarian section and ever since that time she has engaged in various rituals intended to ward off premonitions of impending disaster.

Her current difficulty first began about four years ago. At that time she developed a morbid fear of germs and illness which she tried to combat by ritualistic washing of her hands and body. She became frightened that in the course of doing her housework she would pick up germs from dirt in the garbage can and that these germs would cause her to become seriously ill. Although she realised their irrational nature, these fears gradually spread to include all kitchen work, particularly the handling of raw meat such as pork. This she ascribes to having read a newspaper article by a physician alleging that one could develop trichinosis or tapeworm from handling raw pork.

At the time of admission she claimed to be washing her hands twenty or thirty times a day. On touching anything she considered "dirty" such as cigarette ashes she would immediately wash her hands because of the contamination which might ensue. At home she required constant reassurance from her husband and other relatives that her hands were clean. If they failed to reassure her she would have to wash herself for long periods of time. It became very difficult for her to have a bath, because she had to begin washing a particular place on her body and continue to do so in a predetermined manner. If this ritual was not followed, or if it was accidentally interrupted, she would have to start all over again. More recently her fears about germs and illness had spread to include her children's health. For instance, if a child dirties his raincoat, she would attempt to discard that coat and buy a new one, were it not for her husband preventing her from doing so. Within the past few weeks she had been unable to perform her duties largely because she found it impossible to make day to day decisions about what food to buy or what clothes to wear. As a result she has become increasingly depressed and feels hopeless about her future.

COMMENT:

The general impression conveyed by the history thus far, is that of a classical obsessive-compulsive neurosis in a middle-class housewife. Though always tense and insecure, there has been a progressive deterioration in her ability to cope over the past few years leading to her first hospitalisation about a year ago.

Along with her behavioral decompensation, and possibly because of it, her marital relations have also deteriorated. There is some evidence that her fears and rituals, originally focused on herself, more recently generalised to interactions with her children.

While some behavioral information was obtained in the anamnesis at this stage it was not possible to determine what class of stimuli elicited the symptoms; whether she had discovered ways of inhibiting them, and how germs, illness, food, and clothes came to be the target of Mrs. R.'s debilitating ruminations and compulsions. Nor is it clear to what extent, if at all, her maladaptive behaviour served to alleviate her distress and thereby maintain her symptoms. These are some of the questions to be addressed in the behavioural analysis to follow.

BEHAVIOR ANALYSIS:

On admission to the Behavior Therapy Unit, Mrs. R. was placed on observation for one week. During that time she was intensively interviewed, tested, and systematically observed for the purpose of establishing a baseline of the presenting symptom and to elaborate a treatment strategy.

BEHAVIOR ANALYSIS: *Interview Data.*

On further questioning about the antecedents of her irrational thoughts and repetitive acts, Mrs. R. revealed that she had lived close to her parents throughout her father's illness until he died of cancer nine years ago. Particularly during the terminal stage of that illness she spent much time with her father and was very perturbed by her mother's suffering. Even talking about it at this time produced copious tears and other signs of distress. Apparently, during the last few days preceding his death, her father had a drainage tube in his abdomen and some of the exudate from that tube spilled over on to the floor instead of dripping into the drainage bottle. According to Mrs. R., this exudate represented a potent source of cancer cells with the power to transmit the disease to anyone who came in contact with it directly or indirectly. Since some of the objects in her father's bedroom at the time of his death were later moved to Mrs. R.'s house, she felt herself surrounded by "disease carriers."

No amount of reassurance by relatives, friends or physicians that cancer is not transmitted in this way had the slightest effect on her belief system. She read avidly whatever she could find on the subject of cancer, until one day she found a magazine article which she interpreted to mean that cancer may be caused by a virus frequently found in raw meat, particularly in pork products. Since that time she has not been able to handle raw pork, nor to eat pork in any form. More recently this avoidance response generalized to the handling of all raw meat.

She readily agreed that her assumptions about cancer were probably unfounded, but this in no way helped her to master the avoidance behavior or to lessen the intrusiveness of her thoughts. Questioned about the consequences of her irrational beliefs and behavior, she claimed that they were wholly negative. Already they had alienated her husband and were in the process of doing the same to her children, relatives and friends.

After each interview, she typically asked for reassurance that raw meat is not a cancer carrier and on occasions insisted on written affirmation to this effect.

Only a few reinforcers are left to her. Once keen on movies and social gatherings, she now spends her time almost exclusively with her husband and children. They never go out. Challenged by the observation that her problems may be depriving her and her family of many pleasures of daily living she replied, "Yes, I know, but there is nothing I can do about that."

BEHAVIOR ANALYSIS: *Observations.*

These were made on the ward, and during brief visits to her home. They were directed mainly towards those behaviors known to interfere with her adjustment, viz:

(1) Frequency and duration of hand washing
(2) Content of self-initiated conversation
(3) Eating habits
(4) Activity level

By the end of the first week it was found that the mean number of hand washings was only two per day with an average duration of seven minutes each. However, these sessions were accompanied by much repetitive verbalisation and a fairly complex ritual involving prior washing of the soap, counting of rubs, and a careful rinse routine. At home, she also did not show excessive washing, except when asked to handle certain objects she considered "contaminated."

There was very little self-initiated conversation, but when it appeared, it dealt 75 percent of the time with subject matter related to her obsession. Recurrent themes had to do with spots on her bed, the toilet seat, specks of grease, germs under her fingernails, bird-droppings, etc.

Her eating habits were unremarkable on the whole. She was not particularly selective, but did refuse pork on one occasion. During meals she was seen to be flicking dust off her clothes and once or twice showed concern over grease spots.

Spontaneous activity level was low. When left to her own devices she would spend seventeen out of twenty-four hours in bed.

BEHAVIOR ANALYSIS: *Test data.*

On the Fear Survey Schedule she scored fifty-six out of a possible seventy-three points. Her major fears centered on small animals. Surprisingly, she reported no anxiety in social-evaluative situations. Her score on the Willoughby Anxiety Questionnaire was 54 out of 100. Again on Gelder et al.'s Questionnaire (1967) which is intended to predict the outcome of desensitization therapy, she answered eleven out of the fourteen questions in the affirmative. Thus all three of these anxiety-related tests led Mrs. R. to report higher than average levels of anxiety in situations sampled by these questionnaires. Because prior to admission for Behavior Therapy Mrs. R.'s case had been presented at a traditional psychiatric conference, results from a psychological test battery including the WAIS, Rorschach, and Objective Behavior Tests were available. None of these tests gave any indication of an underlying psychotic process or thought disorder. The finding is relevant in this context, because it is often claimed that symptomatic treatment of obsessive-compulsive neurotics sometimes elicits psychotic reactions (Fenichel, 1945). Neither test data nor psychiatric appraisal gave reason to believe that psychotic decompensation was to be expected as a result of symptomatic treatment in this case.

The I.Q. of this woman was found to be in the dull to normal range. This may have been an additional reason for her referral to behavior therapy, since patients at that level of mental endowment are usually not regarded as good prospects for insight-oriented psychotherapy.

COMMENT:

Baseline data relevant to compulsive behavior is always easier to quantify than obsessive ruminations. Even so, it was possible to ascertain that Mrs. R., during her first week on the ward, devoted 75 percent of the conversation she initiated to "sick-talk" relating to her false beliefs about cancer. It was also observed that the frequency and duration of her hand washings was not excessive, but that they were accompanied by a compulsive ritual. Note that according to the psychiatric history Mrs. R. reported twenty-five to thirty hand washings per day, whereas this behavior was observed only twice per day on the ward. This disparity may well be due to her hospitalisation which removed her from the "infected" objects. Also the knowledge that she was being observed may have altered her behavior. Any estimate of behavior change based on Mrs. R.'s verbal report would have been grossly misleading had she not been observed in the setting in which the results of therapy are later to be assessed. It will also be informative to observe whether changes in her anxiety level are reflected in her test scores, as treatment progresses.

TREATMENT GOALS:

(1) To extinguish her maladaptive avoidance responses to harmless objects such as raw meat and "contaminated" personal effects.
(2) To reduce the frequency, duration, and intensity of repetitive thoughts associated with her false beliefs.
(3) To help this client respond to a much wider range of environmental events than she is currently able to do, so that she can once again experience the rewards of her natural environment.

THERAPEUTIC STRATEGY:

All sources of information tapped in the behaviour analysis point to the greater severity, in this case, of the cognitive (obsessive) as against the motor (compulsive) components of the disorder. This of course, is not unusual in this form of neurosis but clearly indicates that at least two types of maladaptive learning are involved. It also appears from the pretreatment investigations that the false belief system (the carcinogenic properties of meat) is at least partially maintained by avoiding all contact with meat. Extinction of the avoidance response through nonreinforcement, i.e. experiencing the innocuous effects of meat handling, is therefore made difficult or impossible.

Hence some form of "forced reality testing," whereby the client is brought into contact with the feared but objectively harmless stimuli, might serve to extinguish not only the maladaptive avoidance response but also some of the misbeliefs associated with it.

The conditioning therapies most suited to this end are either implosion or flooding *in vivo*. They differ, in that the former technique confronts the client only with verbal representations of the feared stimuli, which he is asked to imagine in a highly fear-arousing context. In flooding, or response-prevention, the feared object is presented three-dimensionally, the client being encouraged to interact with it until the fear produced by the physical presence of the object has subsided. The latter technique can, of course, only be used in cases where the fear attaches to tangible objects. Also it is not practical in situations where it is difficult to identify the major anxiogenic stimuli or where they are too diffuse. In the present case the main source of fear was clearly associated with raw pork, a tangible object readily available for presentation in an extinction procedure. For these reasons, and because recent work in other clinics had shown flooding to be a fast and effective intervention in similar cases (Watson and Marks, 1971), it was seen as the treatment of choice for Mrs. R.

TREATMENT: *Flooding* in vivo.

On termination of the observation period, Mrs. R., accompanied by the change agent, was asked to enter a small room in which there were two chairs and a table. On the table lay a large cut of raw pork, as well as some minced pork meat, both completely covered by a towel. The client was asked to approach the table and to remove the towel. This she did gingerly, while verbalising her suspicions that it concealed something unpleasant. On seeing the exposed carcass in front of her, she slowly averted her face and quietly began to sob. At this point she was asked to handle the meat which she did with outstretched arms, taking care to have only her fingertips come into contact with the meat. Complying with instructions, she now placed both palms on the carcass and stroked it back and forth. Thereafter she would stand stiffly with arms extended so as not to "contaminate" her clothes.

The change agent now took some minced pork, rolled it into a ball, and threw it in her direction, saying "Catch." This she did, and on being asked to do so, threw the meatball back to the therapist. During this activity she spontaneously commented, "I suppose you are doing this in the hope that one of these patties will come unstuck and spatter all over my clothes." This was indeed the purpose of the exercise, and shortly came to pass. When it did, she touched her clothes for the first time in this session to flick off whatever meat remnants still adhered to her dress. Apparently the meat on her hands had become the lesser of two evils.

By now the session had been in progress for about twenty minutes. There were no outward signs of distress and her pulse-rate, which had been 135 on entering the room, had dropped to 110. She continued the meatball "game," and readily made her own meat-patties when requested to do so. After another five to ten minutes of this activity, during which she expressed some surprise at her own acquiescence, she asked whether she could wash her hands at the end of the session. This was anticipated and a muddied basin, containing some turbid water was brought to her together with a small piece of grimy soap.

The purpose of all of this was to induce an approach avoidance conflict and to see how she would resolve it.

Characteristically for her, she first washed the soap for five full minutes and then immersed one arm at a time in the soap solution. This she continued to do until the basin was removed after ten minutes. Throughout this period she expressed mild disgust at the unclean basin and soap. Despite her anger, she reluctantly agreed not to change the dress she was wearing for at least a week.

The client's pulse rate was now down to ninety per minute. It seemed clear that she was able to master her avoidance response to raw meat when asked to do so in the presence of the therapist and that her autonomic arousal level also subsided as a function of time spent being exposed to the aversive stimuli.

Because the preparation and execution of flooding sessions is time consuming and often inconvenient, it seemed appropriate to see whether Mrs. R. would also respond to implosive therapy.

TREATMENT: *Implosive Therapy.*

This followed immediately upon the flooding session and took the form of having the client sit comfortably in a chair with her eyes closed. She was then asked to imagine as vividly as possible, the sight, touch and smell of various cuts of raw meat, including pork. Here again, her first response was mild sobbing followed by rapid breathing, after which she soon composed herself as if she had learned to "turn off" the therapist's verbalisations.

TREATMENT EVALUATIONS:

Following these two interventions, Mrs. R. was again placed on observation. She complained about having to wear the "contaminated" dress, but readily understood why she was being asked to do so. She also thought that she could now probably handle raw pork without difficulty. Put to the test, in one of the hospital kitchens, she did prepare a meal of pork cutlets and actually consumed some, without distaste. At the same time she reported that in her thoughts, particularly at night, she dwelt more than ever on the unclean properties of raw meat. Also her washing rituals had not diminished; in fact they now occurred three and four times a day on the average.

Hence it seemed that the flooding-implosion session had the specific effect of alleviating her compulsive behavior, but apparently at the expense of producing increased obsessive thought content. In view of this result, two decisions were reached:

(1) Flooding-type sessions should be continued in relation to other objects she imagined to be carcinogenic.
(2) Her cognitions should be modified by "thought stoppage" and by the instigation of thought content incompatible with obsessive ruminations about germs, illness, and cancer.

FURTHER TREATMENTS: *Flooding Continued.*

The targets of further flooding sessions were objects which, according to Mrs. R., had been in direct contact with the exudate described above. They included a suitcase, a coat, and a radio, all of which Mrs. R.'s husband was asked to bring to the hospital.

For the next two months, at the rate of three to five times per week, she was asked to handle these objects under supervision so that her reactions could be observed and her verbalisations recorded. At first she tried to avoid touching the suitcase. It was therefore stored in her room and during several sessions her meal tray was placed on the suitcase so that she had to tolerate its proximity if she wanted to eat. Similar "forced contact" sessions were carried out, first with the radio and then with the coat.

Her only response to these interventions was to wash immediately after and to clean her fingernails meticulously. At first she was permitted to do this as long as she pleased, but after the first week, her washing periods were limited to thirty seconds. Throughout this time her conversation continued to be dominated by a great deal of obsessive content having to do with her father's illness and the danger of catching cancer from contaminated objects.

FURTHER TREATMENTS: *Modified Thought Stoppage.*

In the form suggested by Wolpe and Lazarus (1966) thought stoppage consists of instructing clients to interrupt the onset of obsessive thoughts as soon as they become aware of them by loudly shouting "stop." After some training in this technique, clients learn to interrupt their ruminations by simply saying the word "stop" to themselves.

From previous experience with this method it seems that self-instructions to stop a particular train of thought rarely have the desired effect for any length of time. This may well be due to the fact that saying the word "stop" is not necessarily incompatible with the continued rehearsal of over-learned obsessional ideas.

For this reason, the method of thought stoppage we adopted makes use of an externally produced aversive stimulus consisting of high intensity white noise. (Noise generators suitable for this purpose are readily available from many psychological instrument companies.)

The words known to have obsessive connotations for Mrs. R. such as "cancer," "suitcase," "pork," "germs," etc. were interspersed among a list of common and neutral words such as "table," "dark," "slow," "king," etc. This list was then presented as a word association test while Mrs. R. was wearing earphones connected to a white noise generator. As soon as her reaction time to the traumatic words exceeded five seconds, or her association to a word was "idiosyncratic," she would hear a blast of white noise which stayed on until she produced a nonpathological association to the stimulus word. As soon as she did this, the tone would cease. In this way she not only learned to interrupt the pathological association, but also learned to discriminate between "normal" and "pathological" responses since the latter led to aversion while the former produced aversion relief. This procedure was administered twenty-two times before all associations were given at the expected rate and with neutral content. Although Mrs. R. claimed to have obtained some relief from this method, and also produced less obsessional material in her spontaneous conversation, there were still many times each day when she sat quietly brooding about her cancer fears. To reduce these opportunities for cognitive rehearsal of her obsessions further treatment was initiated.

FURTHER TREATMENTS: *Induction of Incompatible Thought Content.*

As mentioned above, thought stoppage helped Mrs. R. to control some of her obsessive thoughts, perhaps because pathological associations were punished and nonpathological ones acquired in their stead. But if this therapeutic gain was not to extinguish with time, and gradually be replaced by the earlier, much stronger pathological associations, something was needed to reduce or eliminate the cognitive rehearsal of irrational thoughts which had so long maintained Mrs. R.'s obsessions. In other words, a cognitive procedure was required that would capitalise on the client's long-established pattern of repetitively associating certain concepts but change the content of these associations so as to make them more adaptive. Such an exercise would, necessarily, be incompatible with simultaneous rehearsal of the previous maladaptive cognitions. In accordance with this rationale, and because Mrs. R. had always had an interest in cookery, she was encouraged to spend her free time on the rote learning of "cook-book prose." Each day she was to learn at least one page, and this was checked out every evening for two weeks. She took to this task quite readily, and brought to it the same regularity and concentration previously devoted to her obsessions. She also took great pride in being letter-perfect at the end of each day and received much social reinforcement for this.

FINAL EVALUATION AND DECISION TO TERMINATE TREATMENT:

After Mrs. R. had been in hospital for three months, and had begun to show some improvement in terms of her verbal and ritualistic behavior on the ward, she started going home for weekends. At this stage her husband had become sufficiently familiar with the treatment process to supervise additional flooding sessions at home with respect to "contaminated" objects not available in the hospital, because they were too cumbersome to move.

The written reports he was asked to make showed that after systematic exposure to the new objects, his wife's compulsive rituals were initially more evident than they had been in the hospital. A note after the first week read: "Home for supper. Wife cooked pork chops and didn't like it very much, but did it all the same." Another note at about the same time said: "She did a very good job. Made supper, used garbage can, washed dishes, and didn't wash hands. A very good improvement." Yet another note, which may well reflect a carry-over from management on the ward, read: "She said to me earlier in the day that there were a lot of questions she wanted to ask, but decided not to." But every now and then it was clear from the husband's report that Mrs. R. was still worried about touching certain objects in the house, because they might have been contaminated by cancer germs.

For this reason the various treatments described above were continued for a total of six months. By that time her obsessions and rituals were hardly in evidence on the ward, and much reduced at home. Self-report measures repeated at that time showed a drop from 56 to 37 on the Fear Survey Schedule, her anxiety score on the Willoughby Questionnaire had decreased from 54 to 23, and affirmative answers to the Gelder Questionnaire fell from 11 to 2.

A progress note by the attending psychiatrist, two weeks before her discharge stated: "The patient has clearly improved. She does not wash her hands more than three to four times a day. Even though she still has some rituals in doing so, she does not wash for more than thirty seconds each time. . . . She has been able to clean her home and was not bothered overtly by fear of cancer related to her father's death or the things which were in the room in which he died. She has been able to cook . . . . She says that she still has ideas of cancer, but they do not bother her." (The frequency of hand washing by the client in her home environment, before and after treatment, is shown in Figure 1).

In the light of this information, all treatment was terminated six and a half months after admission. At first, Mrs. R.'s home leaves were extended to include weekends and evenings during the week, until she remained at home altogether.

FOLLOW-UP:

Immediately upon discharge her husband was instructed to see that Mrs. R. continue the "flooding exercises" daily until further notice. This he did most conscientiously, reporting to the hospital at regular intervals. Though attempts at avoidance of certain objects in the house were initially reported, these soon ceased to interfere with Mrs. R.'s housekeeping activities. She was able to look after her children and began to take some interest in her social environment.

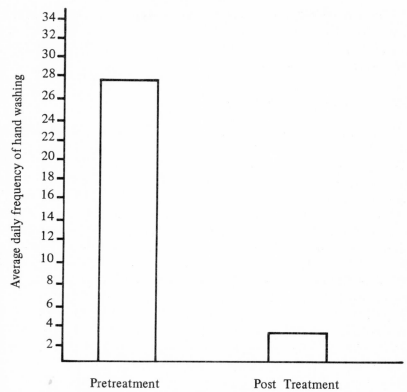

Figure 1. Frequency of ritualistic hand washing before and after flooding *in vivo*.

Because she was alone at home during most of the day she was encouraged to take at least a part-time job, but this she found difficult to arrange. She was regularly visited by a social worker who, three years after Mrs. R.'s discharge, reported that the client's husband had taken to drink and that Mrs. R. had requested marital counseling, which was arranged for them.

When last seen seven years after discharge, Mrs. R. was coping in her domestic role and had a limited social life outside of home. She looked well, had gained a little weight, and was smartly dressed. Her husband reported that there were few remnants of her cancer phobia and the avoidance behavior associated with it. She does volunteer work for her church and is keen on Bible study. When asked to what she ascribed her recovery she reluctantly stated that it was due to "having discovered Christ."

RETROSPECTIVE APPRAISAL:

The case illustrates a systematic, differentiated approach to the verbal, motor, and autonomic components of a typical obsessive-compulsive reaction. It also demonstrates how information from various sources is integrated to arrive at a therapeutic strategy.

The choice of techniques and the sequence in which they were employed, is at this stage a matter of clinical judgment. Some behavior therapists might have used desensitization techniques rather than flooding or implosion. Others might have changed the order of presentation and used flooding only after implosion had failed. Decisions of this sort depend on many variables, including the degree of client cooperation. Mrs. R. was extremely cooperative in that she agreed to participate in all phases of a treatment programme that was highly aversive to her at times. Surprisingly, client cooperation, even in aversion therapy, has been found to be the rule rather than the exception. Perhaps this is because the clients accepted for treatment had been incapacitated for years, and were therefore willing to participate in a new treatment even if unpleasant. Nevertheless, the importance of communicating to the patient the rationale of all treatments they are asked to undergo cannot be overemphasized. Omitting this most important step not only increases the number of dropouts from therapy, but also deprives the client of personal involvement in his recovery.

Another point of general validity illustrated by this case is that behavior therapy of the major neuroses rarely leads to recovery in the sense of total symptom elimination. More often, it achieves an alleviation of the presenting problem, sufficient to enable the client to cope once again with his environment. In some few cases, the renewed and rewarding interaction with others may lead, in turn, to complete recovery.

TOTAL TIME IN BEHAVIOR THERAPY: *Eight Months.*

REFERENCES

Gelder, M. G., Marks, I. M., and Wolff, H. H.: Desensitization and psychotherapy in the treatment of phobic states: A controlled inquiry, *Br J Psychiatry, 113,* 55-73, 1967.

Fenichel, O.: *The Psychoanalytic Theory of Neurosis.* New York, Norton, 1945.

Watson, J. P., and Marks, I. M.: Relevant and irrelevant fear in flooding — a crossover study of phobic patients. *Behavior Therapy, 2:275-293,* 1971.

Wolpe, J., and Lazarus, A.: *Behavior Therapy Techniques,* New York, Pergamon, 1966.

Supplementary Readings

Blanchard, E. B.: Brief flooding treatment for debilitating revulsion. *Behav Res Ther, 13:*193-195, 1975.

Hackmann, Ann, and McLean, Carole: A comparison of flooding and thought stopping in the treatment of obsessional neurosis. *Behav Res Ther, 13:*263-270, 1975.

Hersen, M., Eisler, R., and Miller, P.: Development of assertive responses: Clinical measurement and research considerations. *Behav Res Ther, 11:*505-551, 1973.

Mills, H., Agras, S., Barlow, D., and Mills, J.: Compulsive rituals treated by response prevention: An experimental analysis. *Annual Review of Behavior Therapy: Theory and Practice, 12:*109-126, 1974.

Rabavilas, A. D. and Boulougouris, J. C.: Physiological accompaniments of ruminations, flooding and thought-stopping in obsessive patients. *Behav Res Ther, 12:*239-243, 1974.

Röper, G., Rachman, S., and Marks, I.: Passive and participant modelling in exposure treatment of obsessive-compulsive neurotics. *Behav Res Ther, 13:*271-279, 1975.

CHAPTER 3

CONTINGENCY MANAGEMENT

BEHAVIOR PROBLEM: *Social withdrawal and fear of eye contact*
PSYCHIATRIC DIAGNOSIS: *Chronic schizophrenia*
MAJOR INTERVENTION: *Contingent reinforcement by tokens*
ADDITIONAL METHODS USED: *Relaxation, desensitization, and assertion training*

General appearance, main complaint and circumstances at intake:

By the time this twenty-eight-year-old, single girl was considered for behavior therapy, she had already spent four years in various mental hospitals.

Request for a Behavior Therapy consultation was made by the Chief of Service on the ward where Freda had spent the last eighteen months. She had not responded to phenothiazine medication. Behavior therapy was suggested because she had become increasingly inactive, withdrawn, and difficult to manage on the ward.

When transfer to the Behavior Therapy Unit was proposed to her, she at first refused to go there even for an initial interview. The behavior therapist therefore conducted the intake interview on her ward. He found her sitting on a bed, vacantly staring out of the window. On being spoken to, she barely said hello. Her speech was slow and monotone, her gaze, deliberately averted from the visitor. She was a tall woman, somewhat overweight, with sallow complexion and melancholy eyes.

Freda emitted no spontaneous conversation. Asked why she was sitting there, rather than participating in some work project or recreational activity, she said that she was tired. She explained her presence in the hospital as being due to her parents, "who put me here." On further questioning, she talked about the difficulty she has looking at people, particularly women, and showed some interest when it was explained to her that behavior therapy may help her overcome this problem.

FAMILY BACKGROUND:

Freda's father died six years ago in a mental hospital at the age of fifty-seven. He had a long history of alcoholism and developed symptoms of thought disorder three years before he died of cirrhosis of the liver.

The client was an unwanted child, rejected by the mother, but very dependent on her. There was one brother, three years older than the client. Freda was always very jealous of him because of the close relationship he enjoyed with his mother. He is now married and working for an oil company in Venezuela.

Prior to the father's terminal illness, the family was reasonably well-off. Both children finished high school, and Freda graduated from university with a diploma in physiotherapy. Freda's mother now lives on her husband's pension and has a modest income from working as a seamstress in her own home. The brother has also contributed to the upkeep of his mother and sister, since the latter became incapacitated.

PERSONAL HISTORY:

The mother reports that Freda was a healthy child, who rarely missed a day at school because of physical illness. She was, however, rather seclusive and stayed away from such communal activities as gym and games. She much preferred staying at home, reading or daydreaming. Scholastically she did well and attained high standing, particularly in History and English.

Her social maturation was very slow. She had one girlfriend in grade 6, who was killed in a traffic accident. Thereafter Freda attached herself to no one, and never had a date at any time. Menstruation began at fifteen, but remained very irregular until she was nineteen. Even now, she frequently suffers dysmenorrhoea.

Following the example of an older cousin, she decided to become a physiotherapist, and completed her training at the age of twenty-two. During the first year at work, it became apparent that she was unable to accommodate to the demands made on her. She worked slowly and could not relate to the patients she was asked to treat. She left her job after eight months and has not worked since. As a result, the already strained relations between mother and daughter deteriorated further. Most recently, Freda threatened to do physical harm to her mother who had become very annoyed because of her daughter's refusal to do any housework or to assist in the dressmaking business.

HISTORY OF PRESENT PROBLEM:

According to her mother, and an aunt who had known Freda for most of her life, the client had experienced difficulties in interpersonal adjustment ever since childhood. She made no friends amongst the other children, and by the time she entered third grade, a school phobia had developed. At that time, a guidance counselor suggested a change of school. His advice was followed, and Freda was happier in her new school environment, but still remained a "loner."

At the age of twelve, after the one school friend she ever made had lost her life, Freda became increasingly withdrawn and hostile toward her mother. She would lock herself in her room for hours on end, emerging only for meals.

As soon as she graduated from high school, Freda left home but still could not relate meaningfully to other students of either sex. At eighteen she first sought psychiatric help in an out-patient department, where she was diagnosed as having a "schizoid personality," and given psychotherapy for three months.

After leaving the only job she ever had, she once again presented herself for treatment at another outpatient clinic. By this time, there were definite indications of thought disorder. She was put on phenothiazines and was followed in psychotherapy. Her first admission to a mental hospital followed upon a violent attack on her mother, about whom Freda expressed very paranoid ideas. This was four years ago.

Her most recent admission came about as a result of a very similar episode, and she had to be given 100 mg. Largactil® intramuscularly as a form of chemical restraint before being brought to the hospital as an emergency.

Once hospitalised, she calmed down very quickly and at first kept herself busy by reading, occupational therapy, and outdoor activities. Within the last six months she progressively lost interest in her surroundings and no longer responded to psychotropic medication. She tried to avoid contact with everyone on the ward, because she imagined that the look in her eyes made others suspect her to be a lesbian.

COMMENT:

Decompensating psychotic patients, such as Freda, are generally not considered for individual behavior therapy. In mental hospitals offering a behavior modification service. such clients may participate in a token economy program, but the aim of these programs is generally to improve the patient's self-care, eating, or work habits mainly in order to facilitate their management on the ward.

In Freda's case the aim was more ambitious: Resources were available for her rehabilitation outside the hospital, if she could be helped to overcome her major symptom, i.e. her social withdrawal and apathy. Were it not for these aspects of her impairment, she could probably be maintained outside the institution and possibly even return to some part-time activity outside the home. The usual intake criteria determining admission to the Behavior Therapy Unit were set aside for this reason, and Freda was admitted for treatment by operant conditioning.

BEHAVIOR ANALYSIS: *Interview.*

In talking to Freda, the change agent's purpose was to establish as clearly as possible, what aspects of Freda's environ-

---

*Chlorpromazine®

ment maintained the avoidance of eye contact with other people. She had already stated her personal conviction that the look in her eyes conveyed to others that she was sexually deviant, but now we endeavoured to relate that apparent "delusion" to stimulus events responsible for maintaining her belief system.

As one might expect, this exploration initially led to the uncovering of other false beliefs having to do with what people think of her generally. On closer questioning, she revealed:

(1) Although she had never experienced a lesbian relationship she felt compelled to look at women's breasts.
(2) Some women had expressed embarrassment at being stared at by Freda in this way.
(3) Because people knew of her sexual tendencies they rejected her. Hence she could not look at men either.
(4) Her avoidance of people was directed only at adults. It did not apply to children.
(5) She could not tolerate the sight of her own eyes.

The matter of her sexual orientation was not pursued at any length, since this had already been dealt with in psychotherapy. At any rate she insisted that she craved no sexual relationship with women, but would not feel particularly guilty if she did.

She mentioned that being alone did not upset her, in fact she preferred it to being with people. That such a life-style, if carried to extremes, was incompatible with living outside the hospital allegedly did not upset her. She was content to stay in hospital forever, as long as she could go home for weekends and did not have to work. In short, she gave every indication of becoming thoroughly institutionalized.

BEHAVIOR ANALYSIS: *Observations.*

During the first two weeks before treatment, staff were asked to report on the following:

(1) Her social relations with others on the ward.
(2) Her spontaneous and preferred activities.
(3) How much time she spent in seclusion.
(4) Her response to instructions.

At this stage, observations were to be made on an *ad hoc* basis to provide as unbiased a view of Freda's behavioral repertoire as circumstances allowed. Only at a later stage, when her idiosyncratic behaviors had been identified, were staff asked to use a time-sampling technique in the manner of Schaefer and Martin (1969). This method consists of a checklist of "mutually exclusive" behaviors (e.g. standing, sitting, running, etc.), "concomitant" behaviors (in this case, laughing, listening to radio, watching T.V., smoking, etc.) and "idiosyncratic" behaviors (in this case, asking repetitive questions, smoking in bed despite hospital rules forbidding this, looking at or away from people, etc.). Whenever the client was on the ward, she was observed every half hour, long enough for staff to check and record what behavior, in each of the three categories, was being emitted.

The checklist provided a quantitative assessment of the client's spontaneous behaviors (operant level) already noted in the preliminary observation period. It systematized these earlier observations for the purpose of providing a baseline for future reference.

Inspection of the checklist revealed that during the eight-day observation period, Freda spent 80 percent of her time lying on her bed, often smoking, a thing she had been repeatedly asked not to do for safety reasons. When she was up she sat in the dayroom but seemed to take no notice of radio or TV. As soon as she finished her cigarette she would return to bed. Rarely was she seen talking to anyone, but such social approach behavior as did occur was generally directed at males.

BEHAVIOR ANALYSIS: *Tests.*

Her performance on the Fear Survey Schedule was remarkable, mainly for the items she added to the seventy-two common fears comprising this Schedule. These items were people, hospitals and ice. Apart from these three items, a large number of other items (nineteen out of seventy-two) were checked as being *very* anxiety provoking.

Identification of what constitutes effective reinforcers for a client is prerequisite to all operant conditioning procedures. There being no such thing as a universal reinforcer, reward systems for others cannot be inferred from the therapist's experience but must be ascertained for each patient individually. To save time, it is useful to administer a Reward Survey Schedule. The one employed in Freda's case was a sixty-three item list of activities found more or less pleasurable by most people. Clients are asked to indicate the degree of pleasure or displeasure they associate with each activity by placing a check mark on a five-point scale (Cautela and Kastenbaum, 1967).

Freda expressed great liking for certain foods, cigarettes, music, visitors, shopping, knitting, movies, and books. By contrast she disliked athletics, dolls, and letter writing. In this form, the information is often not directly useable, but it provides a starting point for the hierarchical ordering of relative reinforcement values clients attach to different aspects of their environment.

Finally, the client was asked to inspect a series of eighty-five pictures of human faces, and to assign to each face a "discomfort" rating between 0 and 10, where 10 signified the highest degree of discomfort or anxiety. The pictures were culled from various magazines and depicted the head, neck and faces of men, women, and children of all ages. Averaging the baseline ratings, women obtained a mean rating of 7.5, men of 5.4, and children of both sexes, 3.1. The variability of ratings was greatest for male faces. These test results were consistent with information Freda had given during the interview.

TREATMENT GOALS:

As intimated above, our expectations of what could be achieved for Freda went beyond the usual aims considered realistic for chronic schizophrenics. Even so, our therapeutic goals in this case were more modest than those considered appropriate for most other behavior problems reported in this book. She had been incapacitated for four years, and even her premorbid history left much to be desired. She had ceased to respond to psychotropic drugs, and it was clear that no amount of conditioning would reverse the process of her psychotic illness. What could be expected was a reversal of that part of her behavioral deficit, attributable to institutionalization and the well-intentioned, but misdirected, indulgence by her family before she was hospitalized. Hence the specific changes to be effected were mainly in the realm of:

(1) More goal-directed activities.
(2) Greater social participation.
(3) Increased independence from her family.

THERAPEUTIC STRATEGY:

It was apparent from the start that some form of operant conditioning would have to be applied if Freda was to regain her capacity to respond, even marginally, to her social environment.

The apathy she had developed seemed to arise from an extinction process brought about by Freda's failure to respond to those social reinforcers available to her. With such reinforcers being notoriously sparse in most institutional settings, one might speculate that reinstatement of the client's response to her social environment would also act as a corrective for her self-imposed isolation.

Therapeutic counter-control of this social isolation might be achieved by:

(1) shaping the client's behavior to emit more responses and
(2) programming the client's social milieu, i.e. the change agents, to continue responding initially even in the absence of responses from the client.

If successful, this endeavour should lead to greater social participation on the client's part. Later, this new and necessarily weak behavior, will have to be systematically reinforced so as to maximize its durability and facilitate its generalization beyond the confines of the hospital. Only when that stage is reached, is the client likely to develop increased independence, at which point assertive training may be indicated.

TREATMENT METHOD: *Contingency Management (Tokens) and Behavior Shaping.*

In attempting to reinforce so broad a response class as "activation level" and "social interaction," great demands are made on staff time and coordination. As is well known, reinforcers are most effective when they follow immediately upon the specific behaviors to be modified, and it is clearly impossible for those who dispense reinforcers to satisfy this requirement without recourse to some form of secondary reinforcer.

Tokens fill this need, in that they can be easily and quickly dispensed by all staff in contact with the client, and provide the recipient with a variety of backup reinforcers, according to a schedule amenable to modification by the change agent.

There was ample evidence from observations on the ward that Freda followed no routines with respect to rising, washing, dressing, working, etc. The only behaviors she emitted with any degree of regularity were her toilet habits, eating, and smoking. In other words, her repertoire consisted of activities that were self-reinforcing or regulated by rules of the institution.

A chart was therefore prepared, listing those activities considered prerequisite to the reinstatement of Freda's social independence. It included such items as:

(1) Gets up between 7:45 and 8:15 AM.
(2) Brushes hair.
(3) Washes and dresses by 8:30 AM.
(4) Makes bed.
(5) Reports for light duties on ward by 9:15 AM.
(6) Engages in some form of recreation outside her room at 10:45 AM.

Note that there is no mention of breakfast on this list, because being in the dining room at 8:30 AM was a behavior already well-established in her repertoire.

Once this list was compiled and made known to Freda, there followed a one-week observation period in which the occurrence, or nonoccurrence of each item was checked, but no reinforcements were given. These baseline observations later served to assess the behavior change brought about by the token system.

Reinforcement in the form of one or more tokens was to be given to Freda if she performed the required functions on schedule. At first, during the "shaping" phase of the program, approximations to the target behaviors were reinforced. Once the target was reached, more rigorous criteria of performance had to be met before reinforcement ensued. Initially for instance, she would appear at breakfast in a dressing-gown. Now, if she came to the dining-room sloppily dressed she would earn a token just the same. Always these reinforcers were given along with some encouraging remark, such as "You do look good in that dress" or "you did well to get here on time." When she appeared sloppily dressed, that too would be pointed out to her, but gently, and never without some constructive suggestion for improvement.

The tokens could be exchanged for a variety of back-up reinforcers. Thus being allowed to stay in her room more than half an hour after meals, was a privilege she could earn at the rate of ten minutes per token. Watching television required five tokens for thirty minutes, while thirty tokens were needed to go to a movie. Note that all of these were quite "passive" privileges not especially advisable for her to have, but at the outset of a token program it is necessary to associate the secondary reinforcer with whatever the client finds most rewarding, regardless of its social or even therapeutic value. The crucial concept for the client to learn is that tokens are worth acquiring. To get this idea across, it is sometimes necessary in the early stages of treatment, to associate tokens with the very behaviors one hopes eventually to eradicate.

Care was taken to require tokens, at first, only for those reinforcers not normally available to others in the hospital and which the client could not obtain at her own expense. When arrangements had been made for her to receive no more cash from her mother and once she had spent all of her savings, tokens were exchangeable also for money. Still later in the program when Freda had accumulated more tokens than she could use, other items, such as cigarettes, were gradually added to the list of items she could purchase. After three months of token reinforcement, Freda was asked to pay tokens for her single room. She was also fined tokens for smoking in bed, being late for work or not reporting for medication. The number of tokens she could earn, or had to surrender for different behaviors, fluctuated from week to week, depending on her past performance. "Exchange rates" were always fixed in consultation with her and a number of staff members. When conflicts arose, decision of the majority carried. In general, the procedure followed the one described in great detail by Ayllon and Azrin (1968).

Apart from her self-care and work behavior being shaped in this way, tokens were also used to encourage Freda to look at people. Every time she interacted with nursing staff she could earn extra tokens by making eye contact with the person to whom she spoke.

COMMENT:

Introduction of a token economy system, particularly with adults, is a very delicate matter. When it is done in groups, the change agent capitalizes on the probability that there are always some who volunteer to participate and then others generally follow (for instance, see Gericke 1967.) In dealing with one person at a time, as in the present case, the task is much more difficult.

When Freda was first told of the program she not only refused to participate, but asked for immediate return to her former ward. It took much persuasion and a risky contract to change her mind. She was persuaded to try the new system for two weeks. If at the end of that period she still wanted a transfer to another ward, it was promised that this would be arranged for her.

By the end of two weeks, she was quite content to stay, because she responded to the extra attention received from staff; a very desirable side effect of all token economy systems. This attention differs from the "tender loving care" associated with traditional nursing practice in that it is contingent upon the type of behavior emitted by the client. If others in one's social environment consistently reinforce one kind of behavior and not another, the process of social learning is much simplified for the client. Behavior therapy wards strive to provide such consistency.

TREATMENT EVALUATION:

That Freda chose to remain on the ward, after her initial rebellion, was in itself a favourable indication. But there were many others. At the beginning of the third month on the token system, the client had a severe throat infection and had to be confined to her room for ten days, during which time the token program was almost entirely suspended. In a way, this provided an unplanned approximation to the "reversal method" often used in operant conditioning research, except that it was, of course, not possible to monitor Freda's nonreinforced behaviors during her illness. As might be expected, some regression in Freda's activity level had taken place during the enforced period of "time-out" from positive reinforcements. It did not take long, however, to make up and surpass the level reached before her illness once tokens were reintroduced. Only eye contact remained to be consistently reinforced, even while she was bedridden. As expected, that category of behavior did not deteriorate as a result of Freda's indisposition.

After the program had been in operation for five months, there was very little further change. By this time Freda was making eye contact in the criterion situations, 75 percent of the time. She reported for ward duties on her own initiative and was dressed punctually every morning.

Her program was now changed. She was given a job in the hospital supply room where she had to hand out uniforms and do small mending jobs. She continued to receive tokens for getting up on time, attending to her personal hygiene and socializing on the ward. Reinforcement for working now came from the employer, who authorized her weekly pay check, if her attendance and performance were adequate. Eye contact was no longer rewarded by tokens, but she continued to receive social reinforcement for it intermittently.

TREATMENT METHOD: *Avoidance Conditioning.*

Though the token program had helped Freda to make eye contact with others, she was still unable to face herself in a mirror. Diligent efforts to get her to look at herself, even briefly, were met by immediate closing of her eyes or turning of the head. Positive reinforcement of self-viewing was therefore precluded, and it was decided to try a negative reinforcement paradigm. In this the client was seated opposite a mirror, which could be covered by a curtain. Electrodes were strapped to her wrist, and she was asked to look at the mirror for as long as she could but for no less than three seconds to begin with. If she closed her eyes, or averted her head, before three seconds had elapsed, a mild but continuous electric shock came on and did not cease until she again faced the mirror.

The procedure of presentation was as follows: The cloth was slowly pulled away from the mirror exposing first her neck and chin and then only her nose, eyes, and forehead. The inspection period was timed from the moment her entire face was exposed. If she viewed the mirror for three seconds or longer she was verbally reinforced for this and also received tokens. Ten such trials were run per session, the required inspection time being raised by two seconds every time criterion was reached on two successive occasions.

The rationale for this procedure was to provide opportunities for positive reinforcement of a response she had been avoiding because of the anxiety it caused her. On the assumption that threat of shock would be even more anxiety-provoking than seeing herself in the mirror, the intent was to elicit the less aversive response and thereby avoid the more aversive one. If she failed to avoid shock, she could still escape from it by reinstating the "viewing" response. At that point viewing would be reinforced by cessation of shock, i.e. aversion relief.

Although she managed to avoid shock on most occasions, her fear of receiving it rose rapidly. After forty-six sessions she asked for the procedure to be discontinued, and this was done.

By that time she was able to look at herself in the mirror for fifty-five seconds and the response had been positively reinforced 428 times. She had in fact received thirty-two shocks, most of which had come in the early sessions. One might have expected her fear of shock to decrease once she had learned to avoid, but evidently the fear of viewing had become more aversive than shock and since viewing could not be avoided, without incurring physical pain, she decided to withhold cooperation.

TREATMENT: *Assertive Training.*

Though Freda could now look at most people on the ward with whom she had become familiar, she was still reluctant to look at strangers and left the dayroom as soon as there were more than three or four people in it.

She was therefore invited to participate in one of the on-going assertive training groups. As expected, she at first refused to do so, but changed her mind when she was assured that no verbal participation would be required of her until she felt like it. The other clients were at that time practising assertive responses toward employers (e.g. asking for a raise); friends, (having a different and unpopular opinion); sales people (returning a defective article) and strangers (putting a queue-barger in his place). For ten days Freda listened intently, but did not say a word. Then, one day, when another client wanted to practise self-assertion in a situation involving her mother, Freda volunteered to act the part of the mother.

She surprised everyone present, including herself, with her vehemence in the role of the angered mother and even went so far as to offer the other client advice as to how to handle her mother. When asked to change roles with the other client, and to role-play the daughter, she at first did not do so well. It seemed that a great deal of observational learning had already taken place by Freda attending these sessions as a silent observer.

From here on, Freda was accepted by the group and no longer had to be urged to participate. She also did not resent it when other clients occasionally pointed out that she should look at the person she was addressing.

Her attendance in assertion therapy ceased after two months when she was ready to take a part-time job outside the hospital.

FINAL EVALUATION:

The Fear Survey Schedule was repeated at this time. Whereas before treatment she rated nineteen out of seventy-five items in the category of being *very much* fear-provoking, she now only listed five. As three of these were her own additions to the list, i.e. "being sent away," "shocks," and "my eyes," these conditions were further explored with her. "Being sent away" had become a major preoccupation of hers ever since she began to work off the ward. She frequently sought reassurance from staff that she would not be sent away. As the likelihood of her discharge from hospital increased, her fear also increased and a great deal of reassurance was needed to convince her that she would not suddenly be asked to leave the hospital.

The fear of shock was chiefly induced by a course of ECT she had received on a previous hospital admission. The fear was reactivated by the avoidance conditioning procedure, which, it will be recalled, she refused after forty-six sessions.

From the third item she added to the Fear Survey Schedule it was clear that the thought of her own eyes still presented a problem. For this reason desensitization of this item was now undertaken, but she failed to respond to it, as evidenced by the fact that after twenty sessions she still signalled anxiety after the third item of a twelve item hierarchy.

The eighty-five picture "face test" was also repeated at this time. The mean discomfort rating for female pictures was down to 3.8 from 7.5 before treatment. Male pictures were down to 4.2 from an initial 5.4 and pictures of children had a discomfort rating of 3.5, much the same as before treatment.

These test results suggested that Freda's general anxiety level and her discomfort in viewing others had decreased; but her self-image, particularly with respect to the appearance of her own eyes, remained impaired.

PREDISCHARGE PLANNING:

The client's relationship to her mother had also not changed much. When the mother visited, Freda was often rude and aggressive, so that it seemed unwise to plan for her return home at this time. Instead, a boarding home was located where Freda at first spent only an hour or so per day. After six weeks she volunteered to spend a night in the new home, and once she had moved out, she still returned to the hospital daily, to work and participate in some recreational activities.

Two years after her admission to behavior therapy she was returned to her original ward for day care to see how she would fare in a different, but not unfamiliar setting. From there she was discharged on trial, her maintenance medication being Largactil 100 mg. q.i.d., Stelazine® 10 mg. t.i.d., and Artane 2 mg. q.a.m.

FOLLOW-UP:

For the last five years Freda has been living in various boarding homes. Though she occasionally sees her mother, both agree that they are better off living apart. Freda has a part-time job in a physiotherapy department where she helps with equipment maintenance. The pay is negligible, but the job does give her a place to go every day, and she relates quite well to some of her coworkers. Her main source of income is from social welfare.

She has not made any close friends, but is able to function interpersonally to the extent that she goes for walks, attends movies, and does her shopping in the company of girls she met in the boarding home.

She is able to look at most people when she talks to them, but it is still not easy for her, particularly when she is in a group. She is no longer dependent on her mother or on the institution. However, her slow speech and personal tempo, her constant need for reassurance, and persistent tendency not to take the prescribed medication make it necessary for her to remain in a sheltered environment.

RETROSPECTIVE APPRAISAL:

Two years of behavior therapy in an institutional setting have helped this young woman to live a partially independent existence outside the hospital for the past five years. Indications are that this came about partly as a result of systematic efforts to reactivate her response to natural reinforcers. The major avoidance response maintaining her social isolation was also dealt with by differential reinforcement and extinction procedures.

In retrospect, avoidance conditioning with this schizophrenic girl was probably not the treatment of choice. It may have been the fastest way of getting her to overcome her reluctance to face her own image in a mirror, but when the anxiety generated by an intervention is strong enough for a client to refuse further treatment, the method is evidently counter-productive. It was used in this case because positive reinforcement alone, had not succeeded in shaping her "self-viewing" behavior sufficiently to permit further progress. Desensitization was rejected as a poor prospect, because most psychotics are notoriously difficult to relax. This supposition was later put to the test and confirmed in Freda's case. A more promising technique would have been a process of successive approximation starting with slide photographs of herself, projected out of focus. Freda could then have controlled the focusing mechanism until the slide reached whatever degree of clarity she could tolerate. Each improvement in the direction of sharper focus would then have been reinforced by tokens. Regrettably, this idea came only by way of hindsight.

In mental states as capriciously episodic as schizophrenia, where control by medication also plays a major part, attribution of behavior change to a specific intervention is always hazardous. This is all the more true when various forms of conditioning therapy are used over a period of two years. All that can be concluded from this case is that the goals of therapy and the strategy to which they gave rise may have helped to produce the results achieved.

TOTAL TIME IN BEHAVIOR THERAPY: *Twenty-four months.*

REFERENCES

Ayllon, T., and Azrin, N. H.: *The Token Economy: A Motivational System for Therapy and Rehabilitation.* New York, Appleton, 1968.

Cautela, J. R., and Kastenbaum, R. A.: A reinforcement survey schedule for use in therapy, training and research. *Psychol Rep, 20*:1115-1130, 1967.

Gericke, J. R.: Problems for behavioral therapy in mental hospitals. *Psychol Rep, 20*:534, 1967.

Schaefer, H. H., and Martin, P. L.: *Behavioral Therapy.* New York, McGraw, 1969.

SUPPLEMENTARY READINGS

Bernstein, V. I.: The impact of psychiatric ward programming on patient habitation: The relative merits of systematic contingency management, non-contingent milieu, and no formal ward programs. *Dissertation Abstracts International.* 36:417-B, 1975.

Lomont, J. F., and Edwards, J. E.: The role of relaxation in systematic desensitization. *Behav Res Ther, 5*:11-25, 1967.

Rathus, S. A.: Instigation of assertive behavior through video tape-mediated assertive models and directed practice. *Behav Res Ther, 11*:57-65, 1973.

Walker, H. M., and Hope, H.: The use of group and individual reinforcement contingencies in the modification of social withdrawal. In L. A. Hamerlynck, L. C. Handy, and E. J. Mash (Eds.): *Behavioral Change: Methodology, Concepts, and Practice,* Champaign, Res Press, pp. 358, 1973.

Illustrative Case Material

PART TWO: PHYSICAL EXPRESSIONS OF SOCIAL WITHDRAWAL

CHAPTER 4

COVERT SENSITIZATION

BEHAVIOR PROBLEM: *Excessive use of drugs and alcohol*
PSYCHIATRIC DIAGNOSIS: *Drug addiction and chronic alcoholism*
MAJOR INTERVENTION: *Covert sensitization*
ADDITIONAL METHODS USED: *Desensitization and behavior rehearsal*

General appearance, main complaint and circumstances at intake:

This thirty-five-year-old accountant was referred by his private physician whom he had consulted because of epigastric pains and difficulties in walking. The latter complaint was diagnosed as neuritis. The gastric condition was investigated by means of a barium meal to establish whether an ulcer was present. The outcome was negative, and both physical complaints were recognized as secondary to a long standing history of drug abuse and excessive drinking.

Mr. A. saw his referral to behavior therapy as yet another "counsel of despair," signifying that his condition was beyond medical aid and probably incurable. He had had numerous admissions to various psychiatric clinics and hospitals during the past ten years, but none of these had brought more than temporary relief. His attitude at this time was one of despondency and skepticism. On being offered treatment as an inpatient in behavior therapy, his retort was: "I have nothing to lose."

The verbal statement was consistent with his appearance. He looked tired and emaciated, wore a frayed shirt and his unpressed business suit showed signs of having seen better days. It came as no surprise to learn that he had not been working for six months and had in fact lost his right to practice as a chartered accountant.

FAMILY BACKGROUND:

Mr. A.'s mother is in her seventies and has never suffered from any form of nervous instability. The same was true of the father who was a builder and died as a result of an occupational accident when he was sixty-two years old. He had little affection for his children, of whom there were three, the client being the youngest. Mr. A's sister is married and living in South America; his brother still lives with his mother whose attitude to her sons has always been warm and overprotective. The relationship between the two brothers is impersonal, though friendly.

PERSONAL HISTORY:

Mr. A. was born prematurely and spent the first two weeks of life in an incubator. His birth weight was four and one-half pounds. Though he remained physically frail, he had no serious illnesses at any time in his life.

At school he did well, but describes himself as having been a poor mixer on account of his "nervous disposition." This did not become a problem to him until he entered college to study business administration and accountancy. At that time he began to drink six to eight bottles of beer per day "just to make myself sociable." At examination time, his alcohol intake increased up to twenty bottles per day.

At the age of eighteen he developed an infatuation for a cousin, two years older than himself. She jilted him, and he met his future wife on the rebound when he was twenty. They were married a year later, when she expected their first child, a boy, now aged thirteen. Three years later they had twin girls, also unplanned but, according to his wife, not unwanted.

The marriage was reasonably successful until two years ago, when Mrs. A. first threatened to leave her husband if he did not stop drinking. She did not know at the time that he was also taking drugs. She has now extended her ultimatum to him, on the condition that he submit to closed treatment for alcoholism. The couple sleep in separate bedrooms and have had no sexual relations within the last eighteen months.

HISTORY OF PRESENT PROBLEM:

Following rejection by his girl-cousin, the client threatened suicide and was hospitalised with an acute depression. Upon his discharge, the drinking increased but did not noticeably impair his work performance until he was twenty-four years old, about three months after the birth of the twins. By that time he had joined a firm of accountants, but was beginning to miss days at work because of intoxication.

The condition led to the first of five hospitalisations for alcoholism during the next six years. After each admission, he entered psychotherapy; and joined Alcoholics Anonymous upon the loss of his job as an accountant. He obtained a position as a filing clerk and there were no major drinking episodes for the next three years. Instead, he substituted increasing amounts of anxiolytic and hypnotic drugs which he obtained illegally and without his wife's knowledge. Valium®, Noludar®, Librium®, and Doriden® were the drugs he preferred.

About two years ago he started drinking again, and it was at that point that his wife threatened to leave him. Finally, three months before admission, he again lost his job because of repeated absenteeism. He sought out a physician with a view to obtaining public welfare support on grounds of physical disability.

COMMENT:

The history suggests that Mr. A.'s addiction to alcohol, and later to depressant drugs, came about as a form of "self-medication" to counteract strong feelings of anxiety and interpersonal inadequacy.

Though stress reduction through downward occupational mobility, and no doubt the support he received from various change agents, led him to abandon alcohol for a while, he soon replaced one addiction with another. This was made easier for him by the fact that his wife, who took a very strong stand against alcohol, regarded drug addiction as the lesser evil. In fact she clearly expressed the view that sobriety was a matter of self-control, whereas drug abuse was an illness.

BEHAVIOR ANALYSIS: *Interview*.

To get some idea of the drinking pattern he followed and the circumstances leading to his drug abuse, Mr. A. was asked to fill out a self-report questionnaire and to describe in some detail the most recent episodes he could remember. The outcome of this assignment was further explored in the interview.

Again he related that originally "a beer or two" had helped him overcome the feelings of morbid shyness which had marred his social adjustment since high school. Not only did the drink help him to communicate more freely, but he was also "accepted" in a group for the first time in his experience. So pleasurable did he find that feeling of "belongingness," that he occasionally drank just for the sake of maintaining his membership in that group. At the same time, he claims to have had little personal affinity for his drinking pals, whom he describes as a "crude lot of overbearing flunkies, most of whom never did amount to anything."

He first masturbated at the age of fifteen, always with heterosexual fantasies. Yet women played no significant part in his life until the age of eighteen. Even then, the affair with his cousin was more a matter of convenience than of strong physical attraction. He denies ever having had any sexual interest in his drinking pals or other male acquaintances.

Since his need for alcohol (and later drugs) greatly increased during times of social-evaluative stress, such as examinations or dating, his objective performance on those occasions was, in fact, impaired. Though initially an able student, he barely scraped through his final examinations at college. This, in turn, had dire consequences for his professional future. From his first day at work he felt inferior to his colleagues. Again his alcohol consumption increased in anticipation of interpersonal stresses such as meeting new clients or having an interview with a senior partner. To bolster his self-esteem vis-à-vis his associates and relatives, he purchased expensive property, cars, and appliances so that by the time of hospitalization he had incurred substantial debts.

Mr. A.'s feelings about his wife and children were very mixed. The predominant sentiment was one of gratitude to his wife for having put up with his way of life for so long. There was little affection between them and when she threatened to leave him he did not fail to see some redeeming features in that possibility.

Toward his children he felt guilty because of occasional outbursts of violent temper when under the influence of alcohol. He recalls with particular distaste the occasions when he forced his son, then ten or eleven years old, to buy beer for him at the local grocery store, against the wishes of the boy's mother. The girl twins were a disappointment to him, but he became reconciled to their role in the family as a joy and occupation for his wife. He spent very little time with any of his children. What spare time he had, away from his drinking pals, was spent reading or talking business to local tradesmen. One of these, a pharmacist, became the source of the client's drug supply when he decided to abandon alcohol.

Under the influence of increasingly large doses of Valium and Noludar, his work performance deteriorated further until his partners were no longer able to cover up for his incompetence. By that time, his financial position was such that he welcomed their offer to buy him out and for a while, he worked on his own for two or three private clients. One of these discovered some irregularities in Mr. A.'s accounting practices and brought these to the attention of his professional organization. Following a full investigation of the circumstances, Mr. A.'s license to work as a chartered accountant was revoked. He was also asked to pay a substantial fine.

Soon after this episode, a distant relative offered him an office job involving only routine tasks, such as filing and invoicing. Asked how he took to this demotion, he said that it came as a welcome relief from the pressures of his former job.

His drug intake at this time did indeed diminish, but he was not sure whether this was due to the relief from occupational stress or to the realization that continued intoxication was ruining his life. In any case, the improvement was short-lived. He soon realized that his past and present business associates thought of him as an abject failure; an impression only too consistent with his life-long self-image. In search of relief, he went back to drugs and alcohol until he became physically incapacitated.

Although the three-year period in which he did not drink, coincided with fairly regular psychotherapeutic sessions and membership in the A.A., Mr. A. expressed little faith in either. He was equally doubtful about the prospects of behavior therapy, as he understood it. He readily saw that his addictions were self-defeating forms of escape from a difficult life situation, but firmly believed that both alcoholism and drug dependency were due to some form of "physiological imbalance" over which he had no control. He was also very apprehensive about not being able to obtain either alcohol or drugs in the hospital, having had withdrawal symptoms on many previous occasions. He dreaded particularly the vomiting, trembling, and hallucinosis associated with that state. Only when a physician told him that he was in serious danger of becoming a permanent invalid, did he agree to yet another hospitalisation.

To check on some of the information given by the client, but also because Mrs. A. was clearly a very significant person in his social environment, it was decided to interview her also at this time.

Mrs. A. is a robust lady with a sallow complexion, who moves quickly and speaks with a tone of authority. She confirmed a great deal of what her husband had said, but made much of his inability to stand up for himself in competitive situations. This had bothered her ever since they first met, and she admits that over the years she has had to make decisions for him to the point where she sometimes looks upon him as a fourth child, rather than a husband. She dwelt at length on his extreme sensitivity to criticism, particularly from people he considers more successful than himself. According to her, he is able to express aggression openly only at his children and herself. In fact his outbursts at them have recently become so frequent and abusive that their home life has become intolerable.

At the same time, Mrs. A. did not lack compassion for her husband's plight, which she partly ascribes to his parents' unloving attitude toward him. She is now quite willing to stay with him if the new treatment succeeds in dealing with his addictions. If not, she considers it her duty to separate from him "for the children's sake." When it was explained to her that the outcome of behavior therapy will partly depend on her attitude and cooperation, she promised to do whatever was asked of her.

COMMENT:

The information gleaned from these two interviews confirmed, and enlarged upon, the data already available at intake. It was now fairly clear that for Mr. A. depressant drugs provided not only an escape from tensions arising from his occupational setting, but also made him feel less inadequate and better able to express aggression for the purpose of asserting himself. Hence it was a foregone conclusion that any successful trreatment would have to help Mr. A. not only to become abstinent, but also more communicative, relaxed, and assertive.

BEHAVIOR ANALYSIS: *Observations*

Before admission to the Behavior Therapy Unit, Mr. A. had been taking Doriden and Librium. These drugs were continued throughout the observation period. Staff were requested to report particularly on the following five categories of Mr. A.'s behavior:

(1) Attempts to obtain unauthorized liquor or drugs.
(2) His relationship to others on the ward.
(3) His interaction with visitors.
(4) His eating and drinking habits.
(5) The nature and regularity of his leisure activities.

Nothing striking was noted about his approach to drugs and alcohol. Though it is possible for clients to obtain beer from other patients in the hospital, there was no evidence that Mr. A. availed himself of that opportunity. Nor was there any indication that he was taking drugs other than those prescribed.

Socially he was withdrawn. Most of the time he spent reading while lying on his bed. There was next to no interaction with others, not even with his roommate. When he did sit in the dayroom, he watched TV, but did not participate in the conversation of his fellow viewers.

He ate little and sometimes had to be reminded that he was late for meals and that he might not be served if it happened again. This did not bother him, and he missed meals on several occasions, at the same time complaining that he was losing weight. His mood throughout the observation period was one of resignation and despondency. Mostly he did what was asked of him, but showed no interest in developing his own program of activities.

When his wife came to visit, he showed no emotional response and barely asked about the children. He readily accepted what was brought to him in the way of food and clothing. The only things he ever asked for were books. He made no attempt to be alone with his wife but preferred to see her in the common room where others were normally present.

Throughout this early phase of hospitalization he was restless and demanding, except when he was in his room reading. One had the impression that in the absence of alcohol he was finding other ways of not having to think about his personal problems.

BEHAVIOR ANALYSIS: *Tests.*

On the Fear Survey Schedule, the only items he checked as being fear-provoking were those having to do with interpersonal situations. They concerned such matters as "feeling rejected by others," "feeling disapproved of," "being ignored," "making mistakes," "looking foolish," etc.

On the Willoughby Anxiety Scale his score was fifty-six out

of one hundred. Characteristically, the only item leading to a maximally affirmative response was the question "Do you worry over humiliating experiences?"

Of course it should be recalled that the client was receiving anxiolytic medication at the time these tests were given. In the absence of such medication his anxiety score might well have been much higher.

Since it was clear that some form of operant management, and/or aversion therapy, would be considered in this case, a Reward Survey Schedule was administered. Subsequently Mr. A. was also asked to list the sort of things he found most aversive.

Among the things he regarded as very rewarding to him were reading, cigarettes, and cleanliness. By contrast, the items he listed as most aversive included unclean women and children, rotten food, vomit, and dirty diapers.

TREATMENT GOALS:

(1) To withdraw alcohol and drugs.
(2) To make the ingestion of drugs and alcohol aversive.
(3) To enhance the client's feelings of interpersonal adequacy, particularly in group situations, by teaching him assertive and other social skills.
(4) To help him achieve professional rehabilitation.

THERAPEUTIC STRATEGY:

The client had ceased drinking alcoholic beverages shortly before entering the hospital. In fact he claimed that alcohol was no problem to him since he now finds drugs to be more satisfying and more effective "ego-boosters."

Under the direction of a physician the anxiolytic medication he was receiving was now gradually withdrawn. To reduce the psychological overlay associated with such withdrawal, a placebo was introduced so that Mr. A. was unaware of what active medication he was receiving. In other words, the total number of pills he was given remained constant throughout, and the number of placebo pills gradually increased over six weeks, until he received only placebos. During that time relaxation and desensitization therapy were introduced. Even so, the client initially showed increased restlessness and irritability.

He noted that the pills he was taking were helping him less and less to achieve the "good feeling" he craved. He also realized that behavioral treatment could not progress satisfactorily as long as he was using chemical agents to mask his awareness of those cognitions causing him to become addicted in the first place.

It was further explained to him that his recovery depended on his capacity to learn new ways of dealing with his problems, and most of the drugs he was taking were known to impair that learning process.

While it is relatively easy to prevent a person from gaining access to drugs and alcohol in a hospital setting, the goal of treatment must obviously be to extinguish the craving that precedes the ingestion of toxic substances. In Mr. A's case this was seen as a two-stage process. In the first place the consequence of drug-taking could be made unpleasant for him, thereby reducing his dependence on self-medication. But to leave it at that would be inviting relapse, since permanent behavior change rarely results from mere elimination of a response, no matter how self-defeating. What is needed additionally is the instigation of some alternative behavior acceptable to the client. If the newly acquired response not only replaces the old, but is also incompatible with it, the chances of lasting recovery are greatly enhanced.

In accordance with this rationale, Mr. A. was first asked to participate in an intensive program of aversion therapy. Since he is a highly literate man, capable of responding to abstract verbal stimuli, the method of covert sensitization (Cautela, 1967) seemed indicated. This form of aversion therapy is preferable to physical techniques, such as faradic stimulation, because it is readily invoked by the client himself whenever the eliciting stimuli for his deviant behavior happen to be present. In that way, covert sensitization comes to serve not only as a therapist instigated technique for behavior change, but also as a convenient instrument of self-control.

Because interpersonal difficulties had already been identified as one probable antecedent of Mr. A's addictions, it was felt that the acquisition of assertive responses would go a long way toward reducing his need to bolster his self-image by chemical means. Finally, an attempt would be made to help the client achieve professional rehabilitation, not only because such a step seemed socially and materially desirable for him, but because Mr. A. had already learned the hard way that the practice of his chosen profession was not compatible with drug and alcohol abuse.

TREATMENT METHODS: *Relaxation Training.*

Relaxation training was introduced simultaneously with the gradual withdrawal of all medication. The training followed the program outlined by Wolpe and Lazarus (1966) and involved the gradual relaxation of successive muscle groups; starting with the preferred hand and arm; continuing to the muscles of shoulder, neck, and face; to the other arm and hand; down through chest and abdomen to each leg and foot.

There are many ways of teaching relaxation, though most follow the general principles originally spelled out by Edmund Jacobson (1938). In the author's experience, no two change agents apply relaxation techniques in exactly the same way, nor does any one therapist necessarily follow an invariant routine with every client. This is quite appropriate, because slavish repetition of the same formula — regardless of the client's response — is likely to create tension in both client and change agent, thereby defeating the purpose of the procedure. Furthermore, the way in which a change agent interacts with his client is a function of many variables, only some of which are fully under the therapist's control. Such factors as age, sex, professional status, social skill and clinical experience, not to mention the ever-present imponderables of personal likability and temperament, determine the quality of all social encounters. Hence there cannot be one formula to suit all change agents. Each one must discover the method of approach best suited to the particular relationship involved.

This is not to say that relaxation training is simply an exercise in "doing what comes naturally." Some guidelines are not only useful, but essential to maximize success. Experience has shown that the fundamental ingredients of successful relaxation include:

√ (1) a relaxed therapist, who not only verbalizes the instructions, but also models them.

√ (2) a systematic procedure, not too complicated for the client to
√   follow.

(3) teaching the client to recognize and respond to the proprioceptive cues which distinguish a tense from a relaxed muscle group.

Of these three desiderata, the third was hardest to achieve with Mr. A., because his muscular tension level, in any situation calling for interaction with authority figures, was so high as to preclude any discrimination learning. In his case, two procedural modifications proved useful. Instead of a male therapist, a female staff member was substituted. It was also found helpful to have Mr. A. sit in a reclining chair rather than lie on a bed, as in the original procedure. One can only speculate that his favourable response to these two changes reduced for him the "awesomeness" of the situation, thereby facilitating relaxation.

TREATMENT: *Desensitization.*

After eight relaxation sessions, the construction of desensitization hierarchies was begun. Items were based on fears he had described in his verbal report, the Fear Survey Schedule and other questionnaires completed on admission. Two themes emerged. The first dealt with a hierarchy of situations having to do with "what people think of me." At the low anxiety end, it included such items as "speaking to my wife or parents," whereas high anxiety was generated by the thought of "speaking to a senior colleague" or "going to a job interview." The second class of events anxiogenic for Mr. A. were those demanding that he delegate control to some other person (see also client's response to relaxation, described above). The lowest items on this hierarchy were "waiting in line for a bus," while items such as "sitting in a barber's chair and unable to leave before the haircut is finished" caused him most concern. In addition, he had fears of crowds and public transport which gave rise to yet a third hierarchy. This last one, however, did not require desensitization as it ceased to generate subjective reports of anxiety once the other two hierarchies had been successfully desensitized. This is not an uncommon occurrence and suggests that items on the third hierarchy were related to the first two along the same generalization gradient.

Once Mr. A. had been fully relaxed, items from each of the two hierarchies were presented, one at a time, with the request that he try to visualize each item as vividly as possible. It is important to make sure that each item cue evokes the same image in the client each time it is presented. If this is not the case, different levels of anxiety could be generated, depending on the specific image visualized by the client. If he is then to signal increased tension, or the loss of relaxation, in the usual way (Wolpe, 1958), these signals will be erratic and not follow the usual learning curve.

In Mr. A's case, both hierarchies were mastered, but as might be expected, the first one, dealing with interpersonal situations, took longer to extinguish than the second. Over a period of five weeks fifteen sessions were required to complete the first hierarchy. Items on the second one, concerned with loss of control, were mastered in six sessions.

TREATMENT: *Covert sensitization.*

In the manner described by its originator (Cautela, 1967), this technique involves the deliberate association of two incompatible cognitions. Thus a client is first asked to dwell in fantasy, as feelingly as possible, upon some recent episode in which the maladaptive target behavior was evident. Typically, these situations have an appetitive or pleasurable element which maintains the symptoms for which covert sensitization is the appropriate treatment. After some preliminary training in relaxation and imagery, the client is asked to signal as soon as the pleasurable image is clear in his mind. At that moment the change agent verbally calls to the subjects' mind another image, affectively toned to produce disgust, fear or humiliation. The purpose is to weaken the undesirable target behavior by associating it with unpleasant connotations, thereby changing the client's former expectation of pleasurable consequences. The success of this technique depends very heavily upon client cooperation in letting the change agent know what situations he finds obnoxious to the point of evoking a considerable degree of unpleasant autonomic arousal.

Obtaining the relevant items of information from Mr. A. was not difficult. He is a man of strong likes and dislikes and readily identified several situations capable of evoking lively distaste and even physical aversion in him. Prominent among these were:

(1) Unclean women and babies.
(2) Spoilt food, particularly rotten meat.
(3) Seeing someone vomit.

For each of these images, he was asked to write a detailed "scenario" describing a particular situation from his recent experience, in which he was revolted by the above items. He readily complied with this request and provided several very realistic accounts of recent encounters with each of the offensive situations. The best of these were used in the treatment program.

Following relaxation and training in the visualization of specific images, Mr. A. was asked to call to mind a typical situation in which he had felt the need for self-medication, and to relate this to the therapist in some detail. He was to rehearse in fantasy the entire chain of events leading to drug ingestion, particularly the act of procuring the drugs, the place and people involved, the state of mind he was in, and most of all, the pleasurable anticipation of their effect.

In the early treatment sessions, the change agent would then repeat Mr. A's account of this reminiscence, while encouraging him to visualize, with closed eyes, every aspect of the situation being described. On reaching the point of maximum anticipation of pleasurable tension-reduction, but prior to drug ingestion, the change agent would suddenly talk about the disgust-evoking images, previously identified.

Skillful timing is required for this procedure, which is based on the assumption that behavior change results from affectively incompatible cognitions. Furthermore the setting appropriate to the antecedent events should be plausibly linked to that in which the aversive consequences occur so that the transition from pleasurable expectation to dysphoria does not appear too abrupt or contrived. In Mr. A's case, for instance, the excitement generated by the illegal purchase of drugs; the impending relief from "jitteriness;" and the careful planning for Mrs. A's absence from the house were more easily related to the sudden appearance of unclean people and/or the sight of rotten food than to seeing someone vomit.

Later in the course of treatment, it sufficed to let the client imagine the events preceding drug intake and to signal when the image was clear in his mind. At that point the therapist verbally induced the aversive thought content in the client.

To avoid the inevitable monotony of repetition, it is best to vary the themes from day to day on a rotational basis. Even then a point is reached when the client may complain that the aversive association, which in most cases is quite automatically rehearsed by the client on his own between sessions, has become so intrusive that he can no longer imagine the antecedent conditions with any degree of clarity or pleasure. Generally, that is a sign of progress. On the other hand, some clients complain right from the start that they cannot obtain a clear image of the aversive situation in the context of their addictive practices. In such cases, we have found it useful to alternate an overt with the covert procedure. Thus Mr. A.'s aversion to dirty diapers was exploited by presenting his favourite drugs to him embedded in a soiled nappy. He had told us previously that the sight and smell of dirty diapers, and the particular associations he had with them, evoked strong avoidance responses in him. On more than one occasion he would have left the treatment room had he not been urged to stay. Here again, the purpose was to attach escape, and eventually avoidance responses to drug abuse, by presenting the addictive drug repeatedly in association with objects known to elicit intense avoidance reactions.

TREATMENT EVALUATION:

It was apparent from the nursing notes that the withdrawal of drugs had increased Mr. A.'s tension and anxiety level by comparison to his condition at intake. Relaxation and desensitization therapy were introduced to counteract this effect, and it appears from the desensitization charts that his specific distress was markedly reduced, with respect to interpersonal issues and loss of control.

This sequence of interventions was chosen because aversion therapy, whatever its nature, must be experienced as stressful if it is to achieve its aim. If the tension and anxieties so produced would have been allowed to summate with the inevitably stressful side effects of drug withdrawal, the client might very well have discontinued treatment altogether. Once the drugs were withdrawn and he had experienced some relief from desensitization, his motivation for further treatment was much increased, although the treatment promised to be unpleasant. At no time did he ask for covert sensitization to be discontinued, even though his distaste for these sessions was quite evident.

Appraising the outcome of aversion therapy is one of the knottiest problems in behavior therapy, because most often this approach is used with clients whose symptoms are socially disapproved and self-reinforcing. These are two powerful reasons why their presence or absence outside the therapeutic setting is extremely difficult to monitor.

After twenty-five overt and covert sensitization sessions were carried out over a period of three months, Mr. A. claimed not to have any desire for hypnotic or anxiolytic medication of any kind. He also seemed much calmer on the ward, so calm in fact, that the clandestine use of drugs was suspected. However, a careful search of his room, as well as the testing of blood and urine samples failed to support this suspicion.

To test his resistance to drugs behaviorally, he was offered a Doriden tablet but was told that if he took it he would have to endure the smell of a soiled diaper for sixty seconds at close quarters. He rejected the offer.

He was also allowed to go home for short periods in the evening, his wife being asked to report any drug or alcohol related behavior. At first this *in vivo* trial also went well, but one day when his wife had to take their daughter to hospital, Mr. A. took two beers. He reluctantly reported the event, saying that worry over his child had made him more tense than usual. At this point further covert sensitization sessions were introduced with special emphasis on beer.

The conclusion drawn from these observations was that some inhibition of the drug addiction had probably occurred, but that his still weak resistance was making him prone to relapse, if and when certain situational stresses arose.

For this reason the problem of Mr. A's interpersonal and occupational adjustment was handled next.

TREATMENT: *Behavior Rehearsal.*

It will be recalled that already in the initial exploration the client had emphasized feelings of inadequacy in dealing with senior colleagues whom he considered more able, better qualified, and in many other ways superior to himself. His wife had corroborated her husband's statements in this regard, and also remarked on his striking inability to express aggression constructively. Both of these observations encouraged us to try behavior rehearsal and assertive training.

At first this was done in individual sessions with the client being asked to read aloud or give a short talk on a subject of his choice. Reading aloud had been a particular problem for Mr. A. ever since his student days; it had become a source of great anxiety to him in his professional life whenever he was called upon to read out a memo or give a report at a meeting. He readily admitted that he could face these situations more calmly when fortified by drugs or alcohol.

Even with an audience of one, reading aloud produced vaso-dilatation, perspiring and speech hesitancy. Mr. A. learned to overcome these symptoms in the course of eight sessions. When the number of listeners was increased, even to ten or twelve people, Mr. A.'s arousal symptoms returned briefly but then subsided. Oddly enough, reading aloud was more trying for the client than giving an impromptu talk, apparently because he imagined that everyone was looking at him while he was reading.

Assertion training was also introduced on an individual basis, but after the third session Mr. A. felt capable of handling job interviews, occupational disputes, political dissent, and joining a group of other clients who were role playing. In all of these situations Mr. A. was very reticent at first, and he never spoke unless challenged directly. After about three weeks of biweekly attendance at these group sessions, he began to partic-ipate actively, and as is often the case with this method, he at first became overassertive to the point of alienating some members of the group. Eventually they helped him to express his assertiveness in a more socially acceptable manner.

DECISION TO TERMINATE TREATMENT:

Mr. A. had now been in the Behavior Therapy Unit for almost eight months. Though he had been going home regu-larly for weekends, and on several evenings each week for the past six weeks, he became increasingly eager to find a job and thus once again return home and care for his family.

Contacts with prospective employers were arranged for him by the hospital social worker. When he was offered a position as salesman in a firm of stationers, it was decided to discharge him.

FINAL EVALUATION:

Shortly before leaving the hospital, the Fear Survey Schedule and Willoughby Questionnaire were readministered. On the latter his pretreatment score of fifty-six was down to nineteen; on the Fear Survey Schedule not a single item was rated as *very highly* fear-provoking. A nursing note, written shortly before Mr. A's discharge, reads: "Mr. A. has been going out with his son and by himself to overcome his fear of crowds. He reported today that he had no fears whatsoever."

There had been no evidence of the client using alcohol or drugs while in the hospital, nor were there any reports to the contrary from his wife. The psychiatrist who saw Mr. A. at discharge rated his condition as "improved."

FOLLOW-UP:

Following hospitalisation Mr. A. was seen at monthly intervals for one year. Throughout that time he kept the sales job he had taken at discharge, but became increasingly dissatisfied with the modest pay he was receiving. Fourteen months after discharge, he made formal application to his former professional association for reinstatement as a chartered accountant. A hearing, at which two of the therapists were asked to appear, led to the client's reinstatement as a member of his professional association. When last seen six years after termination of treatment, the client was in full-time practice of accountancy, living with his wife and family, and apparently free of addictions. When asked which of the many treatments he received seemed to have made most difference to him, he unhesitatingly mentioned relaxation training. In fact he still uses that technique whenever he anticipates a stressful situation. He claims that the thought of medication and alcohol still evoke unpleasant associations; he does not feel the need for drugs to bolster his self-esteem.

He has not gone back to Alcoholics Anonymous, and his wife reports that he has no trouble taking responsibility for day-to-day decisions in the home. Socially he remains reticent; he avoids parties and limits his contacts to relatives and business acquaintances. However, he does spend more time with his family than before.

RETROSPECTIVE APPRAISAL:

The treatment of this client was much simplified by the fact that he was well-motivated and had internal resources to an extent not commonly seen in clients suffering from addictions. The presence of his wife and family, plus the fact that he once had a good position with financial security, augured well for the outcome of therapy.

Even so, the treatment took eight months, during which he was relieved from his usual responsibilities and housed in a place where drugs and alcohol were not easily available. Could these circumstances alone have brought about a lasting change? Probably not, because he had been hospitalised before, without much relief. On the other hand, he was not as impaired and threatened at that time as he had been on admission to the Behavior Therapy Unit. That a certain degree of subjective discomfort before treatment may increase the likelihood of therapeutic success has frequently been noted, and is totally consistent with learning theory. In the absence of discomfort there is less incentive for behavior change. Hence it is not surprising that so many addicts who either have nothing to lose, or who can afford to lose without feeling deprived, fail to respond to any form of therapy.

It would be misleading to ascribe all motivation for behavior change to causes arising from the client's past experience. A great deal also depends on therapeutic strategy. If the client can be helped to undergo some therapeutic behavior change early in the treatment program, his active participation in further interventions — even unpleasant ones — is almost assured. Mr. A's case illustrates this principle.

Of the four therapeutic goals envisaged, three appear to have been achieved, i.e. drug withdrawal, aversion to intoxicating substances, and professional rehabilitation. The fourth aim was to help the client overcome his feelings of personal inadequacy, particularly in group situations. Efforts in this regard were only partially successful. There is, however, reason to suppose that continued professional success and increased opportunity for more satisfying relationships at work and at home, may help the client to feel more comfortable socially. Perhaps this is all one should expect of any behavioral intervention, that it reinstates a client's capacity to benefit from the natural reinforcers — positive and negative — provided by his usual environment. Since the client is of necessity part of that environment, he should be able to shape it to his needs within certain limits. In that process of adjustment, the change agent can play an important catalytic role.

TOTAL TIME IN BEHAVIOR THERAPY: *Eight Months.*

REFERENCES

Cautela, J. R.: Covert sensitization. *Psychol Rep, 20:*459-468, 1967.
Jacobson, E.: *Progressive Relaxation.* Chicago, U of Chicago Pr, 1938.
Wolpe, J., and Lazarus, A. A.: *Behavior Therapy Techniques:* A guide to the treatment of neuroses. London, Pergamon Press, 1966.

Supplementary Readings

Palakow, R. L.: Covert sensitization treatment of a probational barbiturate addict. *Journal of Behavior Therapy and Experimental Psychiatry,* 6:53-54, 1975.
Wisocki, P. A.: The empirical evidence of covert sensitization in the treatment of alcoholism: An evaluation. In R. D. Rubin, H. Fensterheim, J. Henderson, and L. P. Ullmann (Eds.): *Advances in Behavior Therapy:* Proceedings of the fourth conference of the Association for Advancement of Behavior Therapy, New York, Acad Pr, p. 233, 1972.

CHAPTER 5

AVERSION RELIEF

BEHAVIORAL PROBLEM: *Inability to function occupationally and domestically due to intense physical pain of unknown origin.*
PSYCHIATRIC DIAGNOSIS: *Hysterical Neurosis*
MAJOR INTERVENTION: *Aversion-relief therapy*
ADDITIONAL METHODS USED: *Relaxation, operant conditioning, verbal satiation.*

General appearance, main complaint and circumstances at intake:

Mrs. S. is a plump, pale-looking lady who appeared considerably older than her stated age of fifty. She came to the first interview accompanied by her husband, five years older than herself. They were referred by the outpatient department because of the wife's complaint of "excruciating pains all over her body." Her physical complaints had been extensively investigated with negative results. She could neither localize the pain nor relate it to any previous illness or injury.

She answered questions haltingly. Often when she tried to say something her husband would interrupt and admonish her by saying: "Go on, tell the doctor how bad it is." When finally she was able to communicate the extent of her pain and distress the husband burst into tears. They were relieved to hear that conditioning techniques had sometimes been successful in similar cases of intractable pain, and she agreed to being hospitalised. She did, however, express some concern about how her family would manage in her absence.

FAMILY BACKGROUND:

Mrs. S. was born in the United States. When she was eight-years old her mother died of breast cancer. The client is the youngest of three siblings with whom she gets along well. Her father, who runs a small store, was married a second time when Mrs. A. was eleven. She never cared for her stepmother.

PERSONAL HISTORY:

Mrs. S. had an uneventful childhood as far as her physical health was concerned. There was no indication of deviant behavior in her early history. She completed high school and took a business course. At eighteen she left home; she married her present husband at the age of twenty-four. There were three children by this marriage, two girls aged seventeen and twelve, as well as a boy aged ten. Mrs. S. claims to have little affection for her spouse and described him as "a simple fellow with a vile temper who dominates me." Interestingly, she dates the onset of her negative feelings about her husband as having occured about six years ago, when her present symptoms began. She also commented on her husband's very noticeable hearing defect, saying that "it makes me self-conscious when we are in company."

HISTORY OF PRESENT PROBLEM:

Until about six and one-half years ago Mrs. S. was perfectly well and holding down a fairly responsible job as a bookkeeper. In addition, she looked after her children and kept house.

Her difficulties began with a vague chest pain. She saw a physician who regarded her symptoms as psychogenic and prescribed tranquilisers. From that time on, the pains became both progressively worse and more diffuse.

Her first admission to a general hospital was six years ago for investigation of an "upper back pain" which she described as being variable in severity. Numerous tests were done including X rays of the thoracic spine, chest and upper G.I. tract. An ECG was carried out, as well as haematological and other biochemical studies. All were negative. A psychiatric consultation was suggested, but Mrs. S. considered it unnecessary and refused to have it.

A few months later she again complained of excruciating pains all over her body and was admitted to a psychiatric clinic where she spent three and a half months. There she was treated by "psychic driving," repetitive verbal suggestions made while the patient is in a state of reduced awareness. She also received tranquilising and antidepressant drugs. At that time she described her pain as a "twisting, pinching, tearing sensation of pins and needles." She also complained of stomach pains so severe that she would roll on the floor and could hardly breathe because of tension in her neck muscles. Again all physical examinations were negative. Also, laboratory findings were within the normal range. Some supportive psychotherapy was given; her condition at discharge showed some improvement.

This lasted for about one year before she was seen as an outpatient in a general hospital because of recurrence of her previous symptoms. At this point she had given up work because of her intolerable pain; she voiced thoughts of helplessness and, according to the clinical notes, showed depressed affect. A diagnosis of depressive reaction in an obsessive-compulsive personality was made, and Mrs. S. was placed on antidepressant medication.

Two years ago she had to be hospitalised as a result of a domestic accident in which she sustained a ligamentous tear in the patellar region and an extensive laceration of her leg. This was surgically treated, apparently with excellent results.

Shortly before her admission to behavior therapy, Mrs. S. was treated in a general hospital for the third time. On this occasion she was investigated because of epigastric distress and hot flushes. Both complaints were fully explored but nothing abnormal was found.

Finally, the patient presented herself at the outpatient department of a large mental hospital. Again she complained of excruciating pains in her neck muscles, chest, arms, and face. The attending psychiatrist noted: "The patient complained constantly of terrible pain, however, her attitude and facial expression is one of *la belle indifference* to this pain." It was also reported at this time that her sensorium was clear, and that she looked slightly depressed and felt tense. During the examination she stated that in her view she was not mentally ill because "my mind is clear." She did, however, think that she was suffering from some form of nervous disease: "maybe it's a breakdown." Once again, all laboratory tests, as well as an electroencephalogram done at this time, were within normal limits.

COMMENT:

Note that by the time this applicant for behavior change was referred Mrs. S. had already had multiple admissions to various types of hospitals and received many forms of treatment including ECT, psychotherapy, and psychotropic medication.

As is often the case, behavior therapy was viewed as a "last resort." That is entirely appropriate in a situation such as this, where the patient presents "somatic symptoms." Unless the possibility of organic pathology had been fully investigated, and dismissed beyond all reasonable doubt, the client could not have been considered a candidate for behavior therapy. In this regard, the present case illustrates the close collaboration required between physicians and behavior change agents in clinical practice.

Elimination of physical bases for Mrs. S's complaints was, of course, not the only criterion for accepting her for behavior therapy:

(1) In the absence of demonstrable organic pathology it seemed likely that verbal-cognitive elements were implicated in the presenting problem and that these had been reinforced by periodic hospitalisation.
(2) That the symptoms themselves may be reinforcing for Mrs. S. (secondary gain?) either because of the added attention she received or because they helped her avoid contact with her husband and possibly others in her social environment.
(3) That the strategy she used was based on faulty learning through modeling by the mother who, it will be recalled, died of breast cancer (Mrs. S.'s pains started in the chest, then generalized).
(4) That many other forms of treatment had been tried and

failed.

Apart from (1), which, for humanitarian reasons served to motivate the change agents, all other considerations were hunches that if correct might lead to effective behavioral intervention. Since the decision to accept or reject an applicant typically has to be made on the basis of incomplete information, these are the sort of issues that influence that decision.

BEHAVIOR ANALYSIS: *Interview information.*

During the first week's stay the client was placed on observation and no treatment of any kind was given. Intensive fact-finding interviews were carried out during that period. They revealed that Mrs. A. strongly reproached herself for having left her children to babysitters while she went out to work. On the other hand she felt the need to work so as to supplement the family income which she regarded as inadequate. When asked what made her say this, she volunteered that other members of her family were "better off"; they had better clothes and finer cars than she and her husband could afford. She again emphasized how much she resented his wearing a hearing aid and asked whether anything could be done to rid him of it. She was told that this might be investigated at a later date.

Throughout all interviews she made frequent reference to her pains which now seemed to affect all parts of the body including her anus and genital area. She made a point of clearly distinguishing between these "bad" pains and the physical pain resulting from the laceration on her leg. Asked whether the pain ever diminished, she grudgingly admitted that there were fleeting moments of pain relief, but that these were so brief as to be negligible. Another complaint which she frequently voiced was insomnia.

BEHAVIOR ANALYSIS: *Observations.*

Also during the first week, nursing staff were asked to keep a record of her daily activities, verbal behavior and social interactions. Night staff were requested to observe her sleep pattern and to report any signs of nocturnal restlessness.

These observations revealed that the client spent most of her time lying on her bed with a "pained" facial expression. When she left her room it was to ask for analgesic medication or to apprise the nurse of the anatomic details and long history of her suffering. In the absence of nursing staff she would approach other patients and talk to them about her pain until they were bored to the point of avoiding her. The only other activity she engaged in spontaneously, and that with ritualistic regularity, was to follow a program of progressive resistive exercises prescribed by her orthopaedic surgeon to strengthen the thigh muscles of her injured leg. Nothing unusual was reported about her sleeping pattern.

BEHAVIOR ANALYSIS: *Tests.*

PAIN. To measure accurately the amount of pain a patient feels has defied the attempts of physicians and psychologists for many decades. However, approximations to such measurement can be achieved by means of a special blood-pressure cuff, which when strapped to the client's arm causes a moderate degree of pressure pain on inflation (Poser, 1962). Mrs. S. was instructed to report at what point the externally caused pain in her arm seemed to her to be subjectively equal to the "constant" pain elsewhere in her body at the time of the test. The point at which she reported equality of the two pain sensations was recorded in mm/Hg. After a few trials she learned to make this report quite reliably, thereby providing a rough measure of fluctuations in pain intensity which hitherto she had been able to describe only anecdotally.

A second technique used to quantify the alleged pain sensation focused on its verbal component. Mrs. S. was clearly using the word "pain" to describe many sensations of discomfort without physical referent (see interview information above). One way of measuring the intensity and evaluative dimensions of meaning is the Semantic Differential Technique (Osgoode et al., 1957). Hence Mrs. S. was asked to indicate, on a seven point scale, her rating of the word "pain" with respect to a series of adjectives such as absent-present, strong-weak, sharp-dull etc. The midpoint of each scale represented zero, i.e. a point where the word pain conveyed no meaning with respect to the dimension described by the two adjectives. A high score on this test suggests that the word being rated has highly differentiated meaning for the respondent.

In the week prior to commencement of therapy she was also asked to rate the intensity of her pain several times daily on a 10-point scale, to test for systematic diurnal fluctuations. This very simple self-rating was repeated from time to time during the course of treatment.

FEAR AND AVOIDANCE BEHAVIOR. Because it was felt that the client's main symptom could be a learned strategem for the avoidance of anxiety, she was asked to complete a Fear Survey Schedule. On this test adapted from Geer (1965), subjects are asked to rate on a five-point scale the degree of fear they experience faced with sixty-four stimuli or situations known to be fear-provoking for some people. She was also asked to take the Willoughby Questionnaire, a twenty-five item personality inventory shown by Wolpe (1958) to reflect changes attributable to the outcome of behavior therapy.

TREATMENT GOALS:

(1) To help the client discriminate the sensation of physical pain from other forms of discomfort.
(2) To reduce the frequency of her verbal expression of diffuse pain.
(3) To teach the client more effective social and problem-solving skills in dealing with conflicts and family discord.

THERAPEUTIC STRATEGY:

The baseline tests having revealed that both quantitative and descriptive ratings of pain were uniformly high, and that the word "pain" produced many extreme scores on the Semantic Differential Scales, it was initially decided to attempt modification of the verbal component of Mrs. S's complaint. An operant program was designed for this purpose, and a verbal satiation technique was also used.

It appeared from the nursing notes that Mrs. S's complaints were much increased following visits by her relatives. That observation, as well as her persistent reports of feeling tense and suffering from insomnia, suggested the use of relaxation training.

TREATMENTS: *Relaxation.*

A modified form of Jacobsen's method of progressive muscular relaxation was used (Wolpe and Lazarus, 1966). Mrs. S. mastered the technique in very few sessions and claimed to derive some benefit from it.

TREATMENTS: *Operant Program.*

All staff members were requested to withhold social reinforcement (i.e. to walk away from the client), as soon as she initiated conversation about her pains. Conversely, they were to give the client extra attention and social approval whenever she initiated or joined into conversations unrelated to her complaints. This routine was to be followed punctiliously except by the attending physician, who was the only person on the staff to whom she could talk about her ills. The physician's rounds, though, were brief and held only once a day.

TREATMENTS: *Satiation.*

While the operant program was being introduced, verbal satiation was also started. In line with earlier work reported in the experimental literature, which had shown that rapid, monotonous repetition of a single word reduces its "meaning," as measured on the Semantic Differential (Lambert and Jakobovits, 1960). Mrs. S. was asked to say the word "pain" as quickly as possible for one minute every fifteen minutes. This was done for a period of two weeks whenever the patient was on the ward.

TREATMENT EVALUATION:

Clinical settings not being research laboratories, it is rarely possible to evaluate the efficacy of one technique at a time. For this reason one resorts, where possible, to reversal designs or multiple baseline techniques (For a discussion of these, see Baer, Wolf, and Risely, 1968). But even when these methods are impractical for clinical reasons, as in the present case, useful trends still emerge simply from inspection of the progress charts.

It was found that the operant program led to dramatic reduction of pain-centered verbalizations in very short order. At first it seemed that Mrs. S. had merely exchanged targets, and was now using her fellow clients as an audience instead of staff. But this was not the case according to the ward notes. Closer questioning revealed that most clients had anticipated the operant program long since and "turned off" Mrs. S. when she began to harp on her pains.

Verbal satiation at first seemed to increase salience of meaning for the word "pain" but in the two weeks following, temporarily decreased meaningfulness of that word, as can be seen from Figure 2. For the sake of comparison, the word "choking," also prominent in the client's vocabulary, but never the object of satiation, was also graphed showing the nonspecific effect of the satiation procedure in this case. Unfortunately the effect of verbal satiation was short-lived, and presatiation scores on the semantic differential were approximated once again, soon after satiation was terminated.

By this time it had also become evident that visits by the husband increasingly upset the patient. With her consent, he was asked to stay away until further notice. By this time the client had been in hospital for two months.

FURTHER TREATMENT: *Aversion-relief.*

Since the word "pain" had an unusually broad connotation

for Mrs. S., it was decided to use a treatment paradigm com-
bining discrimination learning with aversion-relief (Solyom
and Miller, 1967). The client was instructed to say the word
"pain" about once per second for ten seconds. During that time
physical pain was administered by means of the pressure cuff or
by faradic stimulation. Shortly after having said the word
"pain" for the tenth time, and just as the aversive stimulus
ceased, she was shown a photograph of her husband and
family. The rationale for this was to associate the image of her
relatives with the sensation of pain relief. To make sure that
neither the "novelty effect," nor the extra attention she received
in the course of these treatments was responsible for producing
the expected change, a pseudoconditioning control procedure
was used for six weeks prior to active treatment. As can be seen
from Figure 2. the pseudoprocedure had little effect, while aversion relief produced a sharp decline in semantic differential
scores, used as the dependent variable.

After one hundred aversion-relief trials spread over six weeks,
Mrs. S. was permitted to control the frequency of these treatments in the following way: Self-ratings of her pain level were
reinstituted. and at first she was told that on days when she

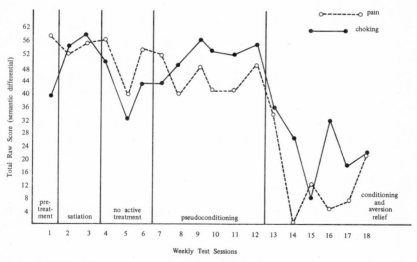

Figure 2. Changes in salience (semantic differential) of verbal complaints as a
function of successive interventions.

reported pain levels below seven (on a ten point scale) the treatment session would be omitted. Later, shaping was introduced so that eventually only pain severity ratings at, or below, one produced "time out" from aversion treatment.

Although in practice, the client could have avoided all treatment sessions simply by reporting spuriously low pain ratings, she did not do this, despite her evident dislike of these sessions. The other control observation available was that her subjective pain ratings did not rise again after termination of treatment.

DECISION RE TREATMENT TERMINATION:

From interviews with Mrs. A. at this stage, seven months after admission, it was clear that she felt "in control" of her pain and the topic rarely occurred spontaneously in her conversation. At the same time she expressed a desire to see her husband more often. He had gradually resumed his visits to his wife during the last six weeks, without untoward consequences.

Because he had coped with the children and the household all this time she expressed apprehension about returning home. She felt he would resent her intrusion. To give her a chance to test this expectation, and to see how she would deal with it, if correct, her husband and children were asked to attend a behavior rehearsal session at the hospital. On that occasion it transpired that Mrs. A. had considerable difficulty dealing, not with her husband, but with her older daughter who was unwilling to relinquish some of the authority she had exercised over the younger children in her mother's absence. It was therefore considered unwise to discharge the client at that stage without increasing her repertoire of assertive responses.

FURTHER TREATMENT: *Assertion therapy.*

Assertion training sessions were conducted, in which Mrs. A. was encouraged to express herself more and more emphatically in imaginary roles calling for directive action in interpersonal conflicts. Initially these sessions were held with her alone. Later she took part in group sessions with other clients. After twenty-five meetings she was quite able to assert herself verbally in a wide variety of situations. During this phase of her treatment she occasionally went home for a few hours at a time, but always returned to hospital in the evening.

FINAL EVALUATION:

Another behavior rehearsal session with her family showed that Mrs. S. was capable of generalising, to members of her family, some of the response styles she had learned to manifest during assertion training. She gradually spent more and more time at home without relapse.

All tests initially carried out were repeated. Her pain sensitivity test showed marked reduction and her complaints about pain had ceased. The questionnaire and inventory results which had given little evidence of psychopathology to start with, remained essentially unchanged. Mrs. S.'s mood was cheerful, and she expressed a strong desire to return home. This she did, nine months after the beginning of treatment.

FOLLOW-UP:

This lady has been interviewed once a year ever since her discharge nine years ago. She was looking after her family, getting along with her husband, and working at a part-time job. She was no longer troubled by her husband's sensory defect and rejected the suggestion that something be done about it. She claimed not to be bothered by it any longer.

When asked how she felt, her typical answer was, "ninety-five percent better than when I came to this hospital." She was unable to specify in what way the remaining 5 percent impairment showed itself.

Toward the end of the eighth year following treatment she noted a recurrence of her former symptoms. At first these were relatively mild. She was given two relaxation sessions and asked to practice relaxation at home.

The reason for her relapse at this time is not clear. She did have a family problem arising from the marriage of one of her daughters, but claims that it was no worse than other difficulties she had faced in the intervening years since her original treatment in behavior therapy. She also complained of having spells of weakness she ascribed to high blood pressure (for which she was given medication by her physician). There seemed to be no other changes in her life situation associated with the relapse.

On the assumption that recurrence of her symptoms was once again related to difficulties in her family life, she underwent stress inoculation (Meichenbaum, 1973). In accordance with this threefold procedure she was first given an explanation of how her somatic complaints might have arisen from stressful life situations even though these situations may now have been resolved. Next she was taught to emit coping verbalisations based on cognitive strategies available to her and finally she was encouraged to practice these coping statements in the presence of a mild stressor; in this case, electrically induced pain. After six sessions, her progress seems to be satisfactory in that she reports less weakness and occasional freedom from pain.

RETROSPECTIVE APPRAISAL:

The case illustrates an apparently successful course of behavior therapy in a severely disabled woman who had been variously diagnosed as suffering from conversion hysteria, depression and having an obsessive-compulsive personality. Most traditional forms of treatment, including hospitalization had been tried and failed.

Why should she have responded to the present approach and remained symptom-free for eight years? Several possibilities present themselves:

(1) By the time she came to the Behavior Therapy Unit she may have reached her lowest point and realized that she must do something about her condition, if she was not to end up as a chronic patient in a mental hospital.

(2) The rationale for all behavioral treatments she received was explained to her, and this may have increased her motivation to cooperate even in a highly unpleasant treatment

program.

(3) The aversive nature of the main treatment procedure may have set up an avoidance-avoidance conflict between receiving painful treatments in hospital or being miserable at home. Resolution of that conflict may have facilitated her recovery.

All these hypotheses, and many more, deserve consideration but they should not blind one to the possibility that Mrs. S. recovered because she learned to label more accurately the experience of pain and to distinguish better between her physical and mental state. This may have been achieved, at least in part, by making it socially rewarding for her to inhibit the expression of maladaptive verbal statements about physical distress.

One reason for using aversion-relief was to help her change her attitude toward her family. There is no doubt that this attitude change occurred, but attribution of it to the method used, is at best speculative. The same could be said of the effects of assertion training, though the efficacy of this form of skills training is by now better supported than that of aversion relief.

Why a relapse should have occurred after eight years remains obscure. It is, however, noteworthy that throughout that period of remission there was no trace of symptom substitution at any time. When the maladaptive behavior recurred it was both in form and content identical to the original complaint. Present indications are that treatment of the relapse will not require hospitalisation and will lead to recovery within a month or two.

TOTAL TIME IN BEHAVIOR THERAPY (before relapse):
Nine Months.

REFERENCES

Baer, D., Wolf, M. M., and Risley, T. R.: Some current dimensions of applied behavior analysis. *Journal of Applied Behavior Analysis, 1*:91-97, 1968.
Geer, J. H.: The development of a scale to measure fear. *Behav Res Ther, 3*:45-53, 1965.
Lambert, W. E., and Jakobovits, L. A.: Verbal satiation and changes in the

intensity of meaning. *Journal of Experimental Psychology, 60*:376-383, 1960.

Poser, E. G.: A simple and reliable apparatus for the measurement of pain. *American Journal of Psychology, 75*:304-305, 1962.

Meichenbaum, D. H.: Cognitive factors in behavior modification: Modifying what clients say to themselves. Franks and Wilson (Eds.): In *Annual Review of Behavior Therapy*, New York, Brunner-Mazel, 1973.

Osgood, C. E., Suci, G. J., and Tannenbaum, P. H.: *The Measurement of Meaning*. Urbana, U of Ill Pr, 1957.

Solyom, L., and Miller, S.: Reciprocal inhibition by aversion relief in the treatment of phobias. *Behav Res Ther, 5*:313-324, 1967.

Wolpe, J., and Lazarus, A.: *Behavior Therapy Techniques*. New York, Pergamon Press, 1966.

Wolpe, J.: *Psychotherapy by Reciprocal Inhibition*. Stanford, Stanford U Pr, 1958.

Supplementary Readings

Ascough, J. C., and Sipprelle, C. N.: Operant verbal conditioning of autonomic responses. *Behav Res Ther, 6*:363-370, 1968.

Bernstein, D. A., and Borkovec, T. D.: Progressive relaxation training: A manual for the helping professions. Champaign, Res Press, 1973.

Drenner, W., Gallman, W., and Sausser, G.: Verbal operant conditioning of hospitalized psychiatric patients. *J Abnorm Psychol, 74*:454-458, 1969.

Kapche, R.: Aversion-relief therapy: A review of current procedures and the clinical and experimental evidence. *Psychotherapy: Theory, Research and Practice, 11*:156-162, 1974.

Rachman, S.: Studies in desensitization: 1. The separate effects of relaxation and desensitization. *Behav Res Ther, 3*:245-252, 1965.

CHAPTER 6

BEHAVIOR REHEARSAL

BEHAVIOR PROBLEM: *Failure to cope, due to inappropriate avoidance behavior and interpersonal maladjustment*
PSYCHIATRIC DIAGNOSIS: *Pathological personality, schizoid*
MAJOR INTERVENTION: *Behavior rehearsal and contingency management*
ADDITIONAL METHODS USED: *Relaxation and desensitization*

General appearance, main complaint and circumstances at intake:

Though Ralph was only twenty-three at the time of referral to the Behavior Therapy Unit, he had been in and out of mental hospitals since the age of seventeen. He was an emaciated, pale-faced young man of medium height. His fair hair was long and stringy, his rather conventional clothes looked neat. His speech was slow and indistinct. The most unusual feature about his appearance was his measured gait and stiff posture. When he walked, his arms hung stiffly by his side and his neck seemed to be immobile.

He came at the suggestion of his psychiatrist at a mental hospital, where he had spent the last three years, mainly as an inpatient. Behavior therapy services were not available there. Because Ralph has a history of pervasive anxiety, unrelieved by tranquilisers or anxiolytic drugs, an attempt at desensitization therapy was recommended.

The client was quite keen on being transferred from the other institution, especially when he discovered that the Behavior Therapy Unit was a very small ward with some single rooms.

He described the anxieties he had with curious detachment, almost as if he were talking about someone else. He mentioned his ambition to become an interior decorator but felt that he could never achieve this aim because he lacked the necessary training and was getting no help from his family.

If he realized why he had been hospitalized so often, he failed to reveal this in the interview. He ascribed most of his difficulties to not having been able to hold a job, and this in turn, was due to his "nervousness" and the fact that there was really no other place for him to go except the hospital. There appeared to be no obvious thought disorder, but the way in which he spoke about himself was unusual.

He enquired at length about how behavior therapy differs from other treatment methods he had known. It was evident that he had done some reading on the subject before he came. His questions were intelligent and to the point. He wondered, for instance, how the items on a desensitization hierarchy could possibly cover all of the things he feared.

FAMILY BACKGROUND:

Ralph's parents divorced when he was six, just after the birth of his brother. The client remembered very little of his father and had not seen him in years. Apparently the father is a rather unstable person who makes his living as a musician and travels a great deal. Ralph's mother had a distinct preference for his younger brother and somehow blamed Ralph for not contributing to the upkeep of the family. According to the client, she transferred to him all the grievances she originally had against her husband.

With his brother, who recently graduated from high school, Ralph is on good terms. They share an interest in drawing and photography. Ralph is apparently resigned to his own failure in the face of his brother's scholastic achievements.

PERSONAL HISTORY:

Since the age of eight, Ralph has been in legal trouble of one sort or another. It began with truancy and petty thefts; by the time he was fifteen he was well-known to the juvenile court. Following repeated car thefts, he was sent to a reformatory where he stayed for eighteen months. He states that ever since his release from there, he has suffered from multiple phobias and has had great difficulty getting a job. He tried to improve upon his eighth-grade education by attending night classes, while working in a service station by day. After a few weeks of this he started losing weight and complained of constant headaches and loss of energy. He was admitted to the psychiatric department of a general hospital where he was given neuroleptic drugs and somnolent insulin. He derived little benefit from these treatments and after discharge spent most of his time indoors, shutting himself off from people. He did not live at home, and his mother took next to no interest in him. In the same year he developed hypochondriacal complaints and attacks of acute anxiety, particularly in the presence of strangers.

The judge of the juvenile court ordered Ralph to be seen by a psychiatrist, who recommended his admission to a mental hospital, where the client spent the next eight months. There he was described as a management problem and was placed on Largactil 25mg. b.i.d. and h.s. Though incipient schizophrenia was considered in the differential diagnosis, he was finally diagnosed as having an adolescent behavior disorder and was treated by psychotherapy for three hours each week. While in the hospital he was up to all sorts of mischief that was mainly intended to "bug" the nursing staff. He was sent home on welfare and returned to the hospital for day care.

Ralph had three more admissions to other mental hospitals during the next five years, being variously diagnosed as chronic anxiety state, sociopathic personality disorder or latent schizophrenia.

HISTORY OF PRESENT PROBLEM:

The client states that his present anxieties about people have to do with his lack of masculinity. He agonizes over guilt associated with some homosexual experience he had two years ago, and he now believes that people regard him as a "queer." Actually, he did not particularly enjoy that sexual encounter, nor the few heterosexual experiences he has had. He became most sensitive about his appearance and consciously tried to project a very "masculine" image. This is what led to his stiff bodily posture, which he affects for fear of displaying movements, such as a mincing gait, from which others might infer that he is "gay."

On closer questioning it became apparent that doubts about his masculinity had beset him ever since his schooldays, when he was teased because of his girlish looks. Much of the psychotherapy he received had focused on this problem.

Fear of crowds and open spaces had also bothered him since he left the reformatory, but had become much aggravated since returning to his mother's home after his first hospitalization. Lately his phobias had become so intense that he dared not leave his room for fear of a panic attack. He had in fact had such attacks and vividly described the tremor and perspiration they entailed. He claimed to be particularly prone to such "spells," when in certain social situations, such as job interviews, parties, or competitive games.

COMMENT:

In a sense, this young man's personal history is also the history of his present problem. The two are closely related. Ralph has had serious adjustment problems, certainly since the age of eight and probably even earlier.

Diagnostic impressions of Ralph, recorded by various psychiatrists, ranged from "adolescent maladjustment," at age seventeen, to "latent schizophrenia" by age twenty-three. The picture emerging at intake, was that of a borderline psychotic. In dynamic terms one might take the view that any attempt to rid such a patient of his anxieties may well precipitate a florid psychotic reaction. Hence one could not ignore the fact that even strong avoidance behavior, based on irrational fears, could be the lesser of two evils, if the alternative were complete inability to cope with reality.

These considerations were fully discussed with the referring psychiatrist and the hospital's clinical advisory committee, which has the function of screening new treatment methods and advising on ethical issues raised by such treatments. It was unanimously decided to proceed with behavior therapy on the grounds that the degree of functional impairment and social maladjustment the client now suffered could hardly be greater if behavior therapy were to fail or possibly even precipitate a psychosis. The chances of this happening were considered remote at that time; and, the more conservative methods appropriate to the treatment of Ralph's condition had already been tried, but without success.

BEHAVIOR ANALYSIS: *Interview.*

The reason for Ralph's peculiar gait and "unbending" posture were already clarified in the initial interview. Asked whether he could walk in a more relaxed manner if he tried, he thought he could but not for long. The fear of being regarded as "queer" was uppermost in his mind at all times. It bothered him in the company of both sexes, but more so in the presence of women. He denied being sexually interested in anyone, male or female, but said that he masturbated two or three times per month. His fantasies on those occasions were generally, but not necessarily, centered on females. His sexual drive seemed always to have been minimal.

The fears he expressed were primarily of an interpersonal nature. He could not stand criticism or reproof, giving that as a reason for not working. People, particularly strangers, bothered him to the point of having to leave any area where there were more than two or three others. He was uncomfortable while making purchases, but could manage to get the things he needed from the hospital canteen. He much preferred buying drinks and chocolate from the automat rather than the coffee shop, though he admitted that the latter had a better choice of both. On several occasions he voiced ideas of reference involving other patients, but there was no indication of a delusional system or of hallucinations.

There were few reinforcers left to him. Sometimes he enjoyed watching a TV program on wrestling or car races, but only if there were not too many other people watching with him. At no time did he care to discuss with others the things he had watched in their company. Drawing was the activity that most appealed to him, and being praised for his creativity meant a lot to him.

He felt very angry about his mother, and basically blamed her for all of his misfortunes. He had no desire to see her, except when there was something he wanted her to bring to the hospital. The only person he felt kindly towards was his brother, but Ralph had lately suspected him of siding with his mother.

Ralph felt rather supercilious toward other patients he had known in various hospitals. He regarded them as less intelligent than himself and lacking in "class." He also thought most of them were coping less well than he did and that they were therefore suffering from some form of mental illness, whereas his condition was a result of adverse life circumstances and particularly, a cold, rejecting mother.

BEHAVIOR ANALYSIS: *Observation.*

Observations made on the ward were highly consistent with his self-report and his conduct as described in the referral note.

His attitude to staff was sarcastic and provoking. One nurse noted, "He has a great nack for making people feel incompetent, unreasonable, and hostile."

Socially he kept aloof. During the first week he spent most of his time in solitary activities such as reading, drawing, and listening to the radio. He made no effort to assist in chores on the ward, but kept his own room meticulously clean.

The only medication he was receiving at this time was Librium 25 mg. q.i.d., which he had taken for the past two years. He was most reluctant to accept any medication on the grounds that it has not relieved his tension and anxiety in the past. About the action of psychotropic drugs he had become quite knowledgeable, in fact more so than some of the junior staff. The resulting one-upmanship was clearly a source of satisfaction to him.

Observations confirmed the intense nature of his social

phobias and extreme anxiety in the presence of authority figures. He would approach staff, sometimes as often as three times an hour, declaring "I feel anxiety." It was also reported that he was restless at night and frequently could not get to sleep. He had no visitors except his brother, who called once during the first week and infrequently thereafter.

BEHAVIOR ANALYSIS: *Tests.*

Standard tests of personality and intelligence had been administered to Ralph on several occasions in other hospitals. His I.Q. was 128 and projective tests, done on two occasions, three years apart, showed marked deterioration during that time, particularly with respect to "color dynamics" on the Rorschach.

On the Willoughby Schedule, administered on admission to the Behavior Therapy Unit, his score was 57/100, considerably lower than one would have thought on the basis of his interview and ward behavior. The same was true of his performance on the Gelder Questionnaire (1967) where only four of the questions relevant to anxiety were answered in the affirmative. The Fear Survey Schedule, on the other hand, reflected the high degree of social-evaluative anxiety so evident clinically.

Behavioral tests to measure the extent of his impairment were carried out in various areas of the hospital, on elevators, in tunnels, crowded places, and in a particularly busy section of the industrial workshop. Though he was visibly uncomfortable in elevators and in the midst of a crowd of students, he was able to tolerate these situations when accompanied. On being sent to these same areas on his own, he phoned the ward from the industrial workshop, asking to be brought back to the Behavior Therapy Unit. He claimed to be too frightened to venture outside the gates of the hospital.

Videotape recordings were made of his gait and posture as he walked down a corridor. This was done for two reasons: (1) to provide a baseline behavior sample whereby to judge post-therapeutic change; and (2) the videotape, when shown to the client, was to serve as a form of feedback to help him realize why other people sometimes stared or even laughed at him. Changes in his bodily movements, as a result of this feedback, would also be more reinforcing if he could observe them on tape.

TREATMENT GOALS:

(1) To reduce client's maladaptive avoidance behavior.
(2) To increase his capacity for social affiliation.
(3) To facilitate his occupational rehabilitation.

THERAPEUTIC STRATEGY:

It was to be expected that Ralph's habitually high-anxiety level would make it difficult to identify specific stimulus hierarchies for desensitization. Moreover, his withdrawal from interpersonal contacts was not entirely the result of irrational fears. A good deal of his shyness was reinforced by others, particularly his peers, who found his giant strides and rigid posture odd and sometimes amusing.

The therapist felt that this "visible" motor handicap of Ralph's would be more easily modified than its cognitive component (the need to emphasize his masculinity). At the same time, attempts to change his motor behavior would probably increase his socialization.

Behavior rehearsal with video playback seemed like the best method for this purpose. If successful, assertive training, covering a wide range of personal situations, would follow. Desired behavior change, consequent upon either of these techniques, would be systematically reinforced by making the opportunity for solitary pasttimes, which Ralph preferred, contingent upon increased social interaction (Premack, 1959).

Once his unusual motor behavior had been modified one might still try to deal with cognitive aspects of his avoidance behavior by systematic desensitization.

To facilitate Ralph's occupational rehabilitation it seemed clear that the first step was to narrow the gap between his modest scholastic achievement and his superior intelligence level. This goal could best be served by some form of continuing education or specialized training. Help from allied disciplines in the hospital, notably the social service and vocational guidance departments, was enlisted to this end.

TREATMENT METHODS: *Behavior Rehearsal.*

This was preceded by a lengthy conversation with Ralph about individual differences in appearance, and how these affect interpersonal attitudes. He was then asked to view the videotape which was made of him earlier and to say whether he saw anything unusual about it. He agreed that his walk and posture were "quite distinctive," but felt that both were within the normal range. Video records were then made of some volunteers walking down the same corridor, and these were played back to Ralph for comparison. He tried to discover for himself in what way his movements differed from those of most others and said that he would try to walk less "self-consciously." These tests were also filmed and successive approximations to one of the "models," who had a similar stature to Ralph's, were socially reinforced. At first he was ill-at-ease during these behavior rehearsal sessions, but after the first four meetings came to accept them as "necessary evils."

Following the initial video sessions, various male staff members were co-opted to act as live models so that Ralph would not simply exchange one stereotype for another. Every time a new cotherapist was introduced, Ralph resented it and made this known by ridiculing the procedure or exaggerating the model's idiosyncrasies. But this behavior ceased, once the new cotherapist also reinforced Ralph's progress during rehearsal sessions.

Once he had learned to move about more naturally within the treatment room, instances denoting transfer of this improvement to the ward environment were also rewarded. Additionally, his attention was drawn to spontaneous changes in the attitude of fellow clients toward him, once they noted that his gait and posture were less conspicuous.

Situational reinforcement, i.e. permission to engage in solitary rather than social activities, was used when appropriate because it was realized that a certain amount of stimulus avoidance was very rewarding for Ralph. When he failed to show up for treatment sessions, however, he was not permitted to spend that time in seclusion.

TREATMENT EVALUATION:

Though Ralph made good progress during behavior rehearsal as evidenced by successive video assessments, the less conspicuous motor style he had acquired gave way to the old habit as soon as he was among strangers. It was as if he were now more concerned to maintain "sameness" than to experiment with new ways of doing things, even if these promised to bring greater social acceptance. When asked about this, he agreed that basically he was not interested in becoming more appealing to others.

TREATMENT METHOD: *Relaxation-desensitization.*

Modification of the motor component of Ralph's anxiety having been only marginally successful, a cognitive approach was tried next.

Preliminary to this, relaxation training by a shorter version of Jacobson's (1938) technique was attempted. As predicted on the basis of his habitually rigid posture, Ralph was not an easy candidate for muscular relaxation. He tried to cooperate, but it became increasingly clear that only minimal, if any, relaxation was achieved and then only in the arms. It seemed futile to continue beyond the eighth relaxation session.

Even so, an attempt was made to construct two hierarchies, one of which dealt with situations in which he was criticised, and the other with fears relevant to doubts about his masculinity.

TREATMENT EVALUATION:

On both hierarchies progress was slight and erratic. At times he signalled anxiety on all except the first item of a hierarchy. In the following session he might not signal at all. No pattern of progress over time became discernible, and this attempt, too, had to be abandoned after fourteen sessions.

COMMENT:

Two treatment methods having been tried and failed, it was decided to postpone introduction of further individual treatments. Attention was turned to his daily routines with a view to testing his work tolerance. A job was found for him in the hospital laundry, but he found that too demanding physically. In consultation with him, it was decided that he should work in the kitchen.

FINAL EVALUATION AND DECISION TO TERMINATE TREATMENT:

By this time Ralph had been in Behavior Therapy for six months without showing any clinical signs of improvement. On the contrary, his attitude to staff and other patients in the kitchen had progressively become more hostile and sarcastic. Quite frequently he would pick quarrels and on those occasions become exceedingly abusive.

He quit his job in the kitchen and refused to take other employment in the hospital. When given the alternative to stay in his room, but without radio or TV privileges, he smashed a window and refused to accept a tranquilizing injection prescribed for him. He also threatened to go home against advice, mainly to do some unspecified harm to his mother. In that condition, he could no longer be cared for on an open ward, such as the Behavior Therapy Unit. He was therefore transferred to another part of the Hospital where more intensive supervision was available.

FOLLOW-UP:

The course of Ralph's illness — the medical term is here used advisedly — has been one of steady deterioration. Since his transfer from Behavior Therapy he has spent some time outside the hospital in foster-home care. After a few months there, he had to be readmitted because of depression and anxiety. These feelings were strong enough to interfere with his work performance, even in the sheltered environment of an industrial therapy department. Various phenothiazines were tried without effect.

Eventually a lobotomy was performed, and following this operation, he reported great relief from tension and was said to have better interpersonal relations, also in group settings. The only medication prescribed was Librium 5 mg. p.r.n. which he was rarely taking.

Five years after attempts to help this client by various methods of behavior therapy he developed somatic delusions; the readmission note again refers to anxiety, tension and depression as presenting symptoms. Further psychosurgery was carried out. When seen at the nine-year follow-up Ralph was still hospitalised and complained of multiple fears. He is afraid to go out, likes to be alone because he "does not trust people." His gait is still quite stiff, and he spends much of his time writing confused notes to his therapist.

RETROSPECTIVE APPRAISAL:

The crucial question to be raised about this case is whether the attempted behavioral interventions in any way elicited the psychotic behavior unmistakably present at the five and nine year follow-up. The possibility cannot be excluded, but it is unlikely for three reasons:

(1) A history of schizoid maladjustment dating back to childhood.

(2) A diagnostic impression of latent schizophrenia recorded during his first hospitalization, four years before admission to the Behavior Therapy Unit.

(3) Preoccupation with his physical appearance, and a masculine role conflict which, in retrospect, may well have been the early signs of a thought disorder leading to somatic

delusions.

This is necessarily a post hoc speculation, but if correct, it is noteworthy that no new symptoms came to light since Ralph's treatment in Behavior Therapy. Instead, an intensification of the anxiety and thought disorder seemed to have occurred over time. Also with hindsight, behavior therapy might have been discontinued, after the major intervention, i.e. behavior rehearsal, had failed. There is, however, no reason to believe that the unsuccessful attempt at systematic desensitization could have harmed the client. In fact at the nine-year follow-up he stated that he would gladly resume behavior therapy if we felt such a course to be indicated.

In the author's experience this is the worst case of behavior therapeutic failure he has seen. Even so, it would be erroneous to conclude that behavior therapy should never be tried with borderline cases or those with frank symptoms of thought disorder. Another case study presented in this book (Chapter 3) demonstrated that the debilitating effect of false beliefs can, at times, be alleviated by conditioning methods. Until better instruments for the prediction of therapeutic outcome are developed, trial and error seem to be the only guide available to the practitioner in treating cases such as this.

TOTAL TIME IN BEHAVIOR THERAPY: *Seven Months.*

REFERENCES

Gelder, M. G., Marks, I. M., and Wolff, H. H.: Desensitization and psychotherapy in the treatment of phobic states: A controlled inquiry. *Br J Psychiatry. 113*:53-73, 1967.
Premack, D.: Toward empirical behavior laws: 1. Positive reinforcement. *Psychol Rev, 66*:219-233, 1959.

Supplementary Readings

Bean, K. L.: Desensitization, behavior rehearsal, then reality: A preliminary report on a new procedure. *Behav Ther, 1*:542-545, 1970.
McFall, R. M., and Marston, A. R.: An experimental investigation of behavior rehearsal in assertive training. *J Abnorm Psychol 75*:295-303, 1970.

Sue, D.: The role of relaxation in systematic desensitization. *Behav Res Ther* *10*:153-158, 1972.

Wells, W. P.: Relaxation rehearsal: A variant of systematic desensitization. *Psychotherapy: Theory, Research and Practice,* 7:225-244, 1970.

Illustrative Case Material

PART THREE:
SOCIALLY DISAPPROVED BEHAVIOR

CHAPTER 7

AVERSIVE CONDITIONING

BEHAVIOR PROBLEM: *The urge to expose his genitals*
PSYCHIATRIC DIAGNOSIS: *Pathological personality, sexual deviation (exhibitionism)*
MAJOR INTERVENTION: *Aversive conditioning (shock)*
ADDITIONAL METHODS USED: *Relaxation-desensitization, covert sensitization, stress inoculation*

General appearance, main complaint and circumstances at intake:

Mr. E. would probably not have come to Behavior Therapy had he not been sent by the court, following his fifth arraignment on a charge of exhibiting himself in public. All previous charges had led only to fines and court orders demanding that he submit to psychiatric treatment. On this occasion the client was given the choice between a prison sentence or treatment in a closed setting. He chose the latter.

For a thirty-eight year old man, Mr. E. looked younger than his years. He was a small, dark-haired man with a ruddy complexion. He spoke English with a slightly foreign intonation, but he had a good vocabulary and expressed himself well. He showed no resentment at finding himself on a closed ward of a psychiatric hospital, manifested considerable interest in a transfer to the Behavior Therapy Unit and promised to cooperate in every way he could. He was most anxious to know how soon his treatment would take effect and whether he would be able to see his family while in hospital. On being assured that his wife could visit him, his tense and morose facial expression briefly gave way to a relaxed, almost cheerful appearance. He seemed contrite at having caused his family so much unpleasantness and vowed that this time he would learn to control his sexual impulses "once and for all."

FAMILY BACKGROUND:

The client was the eldest boy of parents who emigrated from Italy twenty-five years ago when he was thirteen. There was a sister aged thirty-four and a brother, born in the United States, now twenty-three. The father was a construction worker who retired three years ago. Mr. E. described him as a highly authoritarian, but kind-hearted man of whom he saw very little. The mother was of French extraction, temperamental and rather self-centered. The client felt rejected by her all of his life and now goes to see her only because it is expected of him. Both parents and siblings are in good health, and according to the client, have never had need for psychiatric treatment. As far as he knows, they were unaware of his problem and would show very little understanding were they to find out about it. One maternal uncle is said to have been in conflict with the law, but the client could give no further details.

PERSONAL HISTORY:

Of his childhood in Italy Mr. E. has mainly pleasurable recollections. Though the family was not well-to-do, they had their own quarters on an estate belonging to the father's employer. There was always enough to eat, but since Mr. E. was not particularly attached to either parent, he spent most of his time with an aunt who lived nearby and took care of him.

By the age of eleven, he recalls masturbating two to three times per day. The following year he first exhibited to a girl cousin. Although her back was turned to him, he remembers the thrill associated with that experience.

At school he did well; but because he was physically undersized, he was not good at sports and therefore not too popular with his own age-group. He became more and more of a recluse, particularly after immigrating to the United States, where he was often ridiculed because of his poor English.

In transferring from one country to another he lost a year at school and resented more than ever his father's decision to leave Italy. He managed to finish high school and went to work immediately as a packer in a grocery store. From there he was eventually promoted to the merchandising department, and when his aunt in Italy died leaving him her savings, he was able to open a small grocery store together with another Italian immigrant whom he had known at work.

He recalls very little about his adolescent sexual adjustment except that he masturbated frequently and always in greatest secrecy. He was deeply troubled about the possible effects of this, but had no one with whom to discuss the matter. Neither parents ever talked about sex; he too, came to regard it as an unmentionable subject.

At the age of eighteen he met his present wife. He vividly remembers that after taking her home from a date one evening, he walked down the street with his zipper undone. Again he commented on the thrill it gave him when two girls at the bus stop evidently noticed his open zip-fastener with some excitement.

By the time of his engagement at the age of twenty-three he had had no intimate relations with any girl. When he did convince his fiancee to have intercourse with him, he found her cold and unresponsive. She remained that way after they were married, six months later. At no time did he experience full satisfaction in sexual relations with his wife, and he claims this made him doubt his manhood and feel uncomfortable and inferior in the presence of women generally.

They had one son, now aged fourteen, to whom both parents are very attached. Mr. E. would have liked more children; but his wife, having had a difficult labor with their first child, felt that "she could not go through this again."

The client and his family lived comfortably in a middle-class neighbourhood. They were regular church-goers, the wife having become Catholic at the time of their marriage. They had few close friends. Both enjoyed bowling and outdoor activities.

HISTORY OF PRESENT PROBLEM:

By the time Mr. E. reached his early twenties, he was exhib-

iting up to ten times a day. At first he did this very surrep-
titiously, standing with an open dressing-gown near a window
where he could be seen by people walking along the street
below. In summer he would sit in his parked car exposing
himself to women sitting on their balconies. Eventually his
deviant practices became bolder, until one day he followed a
young woman into an apartment building and then masturbated so that she could see him in a mirror as she ap-
proached the elevator. She notified the janitor, who in turn
called the police. This led to the first of many arrests, but since
no formal charge was laid, he was only detained briefly and
placed on probation. This happened shortly before he was married.

After his marriage, the urge to exhibit temporarily
diminished, but when it returned, the guilt feelings generated
by this misdemeanour greatly increased. After his second arrest,
when his wife became aware of his problem, she prevailed
upon him to seek professional help. At first he turned to a
social worker he had known in a community center near his
first place of work. She referred him to a colleague doing case
work in a psychiatric hospital. Eventually, after yet another
confrontation with the police, he was ordered to see a psychiatrist. This practitioner saw both the client and his wife at fairly
regular intervals for six years. According to the client, his marriage would long since have ended in divorce had it not been
for the professional assistance they received.

But despite improved marital relations which apparently re-
sulted from psychotherapy, the deviant sexual urges remained.
At no time did he desist from exhibiting for longer than six
months.

Because Mr. E. was in treatment throughout all these years,
none of the court cases — of which there were several — even-
tuated in imprisonment. When last apprehended, two weeks
before admission to the Behavior Therapy Unit, Mr. E. was
exhibiting near the ladies' toilet of a large department store. He
spent some days in jail and was brought to the hospital in a
police car.

COMMENT:

Cases "sentenced" to treatment by the court, easily create ethical problems for change agents who believe that those of legal age, and in possession of their faculties, should only be treated at their own request. In the present case, that request was made under duress. In essence, of course, almost every request for behavior modification is made under some degree of pressure since few clients seek treatment unless they feel that some aspect of their behavior is objectionable to themselves or others. Hence the essential difference between voluntary and court cases is not the presence or absence of duress, but its nature and origin. When pressure to seek treatment originates from a social agency, such as a court of law, it is assumed that the client is either unable to make decisions in his own best interest, or insufficiently responsive to the effect of his behavior on others. In Mr. E.'s case, neither assumption is fully justified. He had long ago sought treatment on his own, but since that treatment failed to protect others from the effect of his deviant behavior, he was now given the choice between two forms of constraint on his freedom. He chose the hospital; once there, he could accept or reject behavior therapy. His private psychiatrist recommended behavior therapy because she felt that traditional, psychodynamically oriented methods had failed in this case. The client, however, was still free to act or not to act on her advice. Great care was taken initially, to explain these circumstances to him. Not to do so, would indeed have been unethical and would most probably have had a negative effect on his motivation for treatment.

BEHAVIOR ANALYSIS: *Interview.*

Extensive interviews were conducted, both with the client and his wife. The focus of these interviews was to establish in what way their marital relationship contributed to the husband's sexual difficulties. At first it seemed strange that this attractive young woman should stay with her husband throughout so many years, in which her life and that of her son was repeatedly marred by the husband's inability, or unwillingness, to control his deviant sexual impulses.

It soon transpired that Mrs. E. had a clear understanding of her husband's problem, and regarding it as a form of curable illness, saw it as her mission in life to help him overcome his difficulties. She described him as a good husband, father and provider. Though clearly worried by his present plight and its possible consequences for her future, she saw no reason to give up and expressed the view that without her support he would almost certainly not recover.

He, in turn, spoke of his wife in the highest terms and repeatedly emphasized how unworthy he was of her affection and continued moral support. Only later did he let it appear that he considered his wife too inhibited and conventional as a sexual partner and that no experience with her came close to the excitement he felt when exhibiting to other women. He also stated that he frequently indulged in masturbation, always with fantasies of other women. Sometimes these were women he had seen recently, or exhibited to in the past. The type of woman he found most stimulating had those physical characteristics commonly associated with Italian women. His wife, by contrast, was distinctly Nordic, both in temperament and appearance. Asked to rank his relative preference for different forms of sexual practice, he listed exhibitionism as most satisfying, intercourse next, and masturbation least. He expressed strong disapproval of extramarital relations and denied ever having had any. He also denied ever having felt physically attracted to members of his own sex.

Verbally, he condemned the practice of exhibitionism as morally reprehensible, wrongful, and "sick." At the same time he could offer no explanation for his frequent indulgence in that habit. He vaguely believed that it had something to do with his puritanical upbringing and the fact that as a young man, he had had no competing sexual experiences. The only related sensations he knew were intercourse with his wife and masturbation. At a later interview, he reluctantly admitted that he had tried having intercourse with a prostitute, but had not found it at all satisfying.

Attempts to relate the occurrence of his exhibitionism to concurrent life situations were only partially successful. Most often a frustrating experience at home or at work set off a chain of events leading to the deviant act. Since he had a fairly high aspiration level for a man in his walk of life, he frequently encountered frustrations. When he felt like a failure he would become depressed, and exhibiting could sometimes restore his self-esteem. At other times he looked upon his symptom as an act of despair and the possibility of incarceration as a form of escape from unbearable pressures in everyday life. In this context it also came to light that he had once before been admitted to a psychiatric hospital because of a depressive mood disorder and had received antidepressant medication for some time after.

As mentioned earlier, his motivation for treatment was extremely high. He was most concerned about the outcome of his court case which was to be heard in six weeks time, and said he would undergo any form of treatment, no matter how unpleasant, if it would help him to overcome his sexual deviation. He was told that no guarantee could be given that any currently available form of treatment would be effective, and that a great deal would depend on his own efforts. When the rationale of aversion treatment was explained to him, he did not flinch. To test his motivation still further, he was asked whether he would still be willing to undergo this form of therapy even if it were to leave him impotent. He replied that this would not deter him.

BEHAVIOR ANALYSIS: *Observations.*

Because of the legal implications of this case, the client was instructed never to leave the ward without notifying staff of his destination. He was permitted short outings within the hospital grounds, but could not leave the hospital unaccompanied. At no time did he offend against these regulations and his social interaction with staff and other clients was exemplary. He was cooperative, courteous, and genuinely grateful for what was being done on his behalf. During the two-week observation period there were no attempts to exhibit, despite many opportunities to do so, especially at night when there was generally only one nurse on duty. He kept in touch with his family by phone and also with his business partner. There were frequent visits from his wife.

His toilet and eating habits were unremarkable. He was clean about his person and kept his room tidy. When asked to be given something to do, he was assigned to the storeroom where he helped with the inventory and various odd jobs. His supervisor spoke highly of Mr. E.'s industry and conscientiousness. No untoward incidents of any sort were reported about the client's conduct from any part of the hospital.

BEHAVIOR ANALYSIS: *Tests.*

Because an EEG done two years earlier showed some left temporal lobe dysrhythmia, another EEG was done at this time. It was found to be within normal limits. Likewise a Wechsler Memory Scale and Bender Gestalt Test gave no indication of central organic impairment.

Anxiety level, as estimated from the Willoughby Questionnaire, was above average but not markedly so; on the Eysenck Personality Inventory the profile was that of an introverted neurotic. His replies to the Fear Survey Schedule showed great internal consistency, in that all items checked as most fear-provoking, were in the "social-evaluative" category, e.g. "public speaking," "failure," "being criticized."

Since none of these tests bear directly on the disorder to be treated, a more behavioral technique was devised. Mrs. E. was asked to provide a series of color slides of herself in as many alluring poses as she could accumulate. These were randomly interspersed between similar slides of other women. The client was asked to view these slides at leisure, and to activate the slide changer himself whenever he had seen enough of a particular slide. The time he spent viewing these slides was recorded, and the percentage of time spent viewing "wife slides" was calculated.

The total series contained as many "wife slides" as slides of other women, so that if viewing time were randomly distributed he would have spent fifty percent of his time viewing "wife slides." In the nature of things no such random distribution was expected. The purpose was to establish a pretreatment baseline, so that possible changes in that distribution, as a function of treatment could later be assessed.

As can be seen from Figure 3 (baseline) the average time spent looking at "wife slides" in the pretreatment phase was 33.35 percent of total viewing time.

TREATMENT GOALS:

(1) To extinguish those sexual fantasies which, by virtue of the pleasurable anticipation they arouse, maintain the client's urge to exhibit.
(2) To make the act of exhibiting aversive.
(3) To strengthen the client's prosocial sexual behavior.
(4) To increase his stress tolerance.

THERAPEUTIC STRATEGY:

To achieve the first two treatment goals, and to achieve them quickly, some form of aversion therapy suggested itself. But before any unpleasant intervention such as electrical or chemical aversion is instigated, more conservative measures should always be considered.

In the present case, one could very cogently argue that Mr. E.'s low frustration tolerance, eroded self-image or sexual maladjustment in marriage are at the root of the trouble and should therefore be the focus of treatment. But alleviation of just these problems had been the goal of psychotherapy for six years without appreciably affecting the target symptom as was apparent from the client's history.

With some reformulation of these problems, in behavioral terms, one could attempt to modify frustration tolerance by differential reinforcement of aspiration level, improve the client's self-image by Rational Emotive Psychotherapy (by some regarded as a form of behavior therapy, e.g. Eysenck,

1964) or increase the marital partners' communication about sexual matters by means of modeling or behavior rehearsal. But these methods are slow at best, and with the exception of Rational Emotive Therapy, they are still very much at the exploratory stage. Even if these strategies were used there is no certainty that the target symptom would yield to them, any more than it did to traditional psychotherapy.

In Mr. E.'s case speedy results were of the essence, because his court hearing was to take place within six weeks. Unless some tangible evidence of therapeutic change could be obtained by then, he would probably receive a prison sentence. This consideration favoured the use of aversive deconditioning.

There is yet another reason for the choice of aversion techniques in treating antisocial behavior. Opportunities for monitoring sexually deviant behavior on a relatively small, active treatment ward are limited because of the clinical atmosphere and almost ubiquitous presence of other clients. It is therefore necessary to give the client occasional leave, *on trial* from the hospital. This is always hazardous, but less so, when it comes after a course of aversion treatment in which an unpleasant association with the formerly gratifying behavior has already been established. If these "test" outings are delayed too long, one courts not only the danger of producing institutionalization but may also uselessly pursue an intervention which should have been modified or abandoned long ago.

For these reasons the strategy adopted in Mr. E.'s case was to produce immediate inhibition of his major symptom by shock aversion, and then to consolidate this change by use of covert sensitization and stress inoculation.

TREATMENT METHODS: *Shock Aversion.*

The interview with the client gave reason to believe that certain fantasies usher in the sexual arousal leading him to exhibit. Hence the consummatory act would be expected to reinforce the initial fantasy and thereby increase the likelihood of its recurrence. One reason for using shock aversion was to break this chain of events. Since it is easier to manipulate a client's arousal level than his fantasies, it was attempted to reduce Mr. E.'s level of sexual arousal prior to replacing his deviant sexual fantasies by prosocial ones. This was accomplished by giving him Mellaril®, a drug known to reduce sexual drive, and to inhibit ejaculation. To monitor its effect, use was made of the client's own report that he masturbated daily, while on the ward. He was asked henceforth, to provide a daily rating of the degree of pleasure he derived from his auto-erotic practices.

As expected, the client experienced less and less sexual arousal, and after two weeks reported that he was incapable of achieving orgasm. He was aware that his inability to perform sexually was, at least partially, due to the effect of medication, which was discontinued at this stage.

Various forms of aversion therapy were considered at this point. In accordance with observations published by Rachman and Teasdale (1969) electrical aversion therapy was chosen. The source of shock was a transistorized generator, energized by a 12-volt car battery. It was capable of output in the range of 0 to 40 milliamps. Copper electrodes 1 inch in diameter were used. Various electrode placements were tried, with a view to making the experience as aversive, but also as "target relevant" as possible. With this in mind it was decided to place the electrodes two inches apart on the client's groin.

In an effort to time the shock so that it would occur at a high level of sexual arousal, but prior to orgasm, the client was positioned in front of a one-way screen through which he could see the adjacent room. Behind him stood a folding screen to provide some measure of privacy, and to make the shock apparatus less obtrusive.

He was now asked to act as if he were about to exhibit through a shop window, an experience he frequently had in the past. As was his practice on these occasions, he started to masturbate. As his breathing became more rapid and his movements faster, the therapist activated a concealed buzzer to sound in the adjoining room. This was the signal for a young woman confederate, to appear on the other side of the one-way screen, and there to act as if she were confronted by an exhibitionist.

The role required some dramatic talent, since all she actually saw was, of course, her own reflection in the mirror. Within three seconds of her appearance the client received the shock which was automatically timed to last one second. He was asked to report whether he still felt aroused. If he answered in the affirmative, the procedure was immediately repeated. On the average, he received three shocks per session, four times a week for three weeks. By that time, he reported difficulty in producing an erection — even before the first shock in a session. Treatment was terminated at that point.

Instead, the "wife slide" technique, originally used to determine pretreatment inspection times, was reintroduced. On the basis of inspection times previously recorded, two parallel sets of slides were prepared, so that each tray contained an equal number of "wife" slides and slides of other women. They were selected in such a way that pretreatment inspection times for all slides were about equal.

As an exercise in discrimination learning, one slide tray was now presented so that some pictures of other women, but never the pictures of his wife, were followed by shock. As before, the client controlled the slide changer. Only 50 percent of the slides of other women were followed by shock, but the order was random, so that the client had no way of predicting which particular slide would be shocked. Also the shock could be delivered at any time before the slide was turned off, though in practice it generally occurred from one to five seconds after the slide appeared.

TREATMENT EVALUATION I:

As can be seen from Figure 3 (treatment phase) the client slowly learned that "wife slides" were not only safer to inspect than slides of other women, but what is more important, he discovered that "wife slides" were a source of aversion relief. In other words, viewing "wife slides" meant "time out" from shock. It is important to note that shocked slides, in the treatment tray, were never the same as the "other women" slides in the test tray. In spite of this, inspection times for "wife

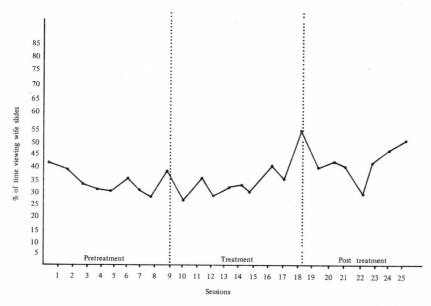

Figure 3. Changes in inspection time of "wife slides" by an exhibitionist before, during, and after aversion therapy.

slides" in the test tray, rose from 43 percent pretreatment to 55 percent after nine shock aversion sessions. As expected, the client's increased attention to "wife slides" was not fully maintained in the immediate post-treatment phase but, on the average, still remained slightly higher than before treatment.

When the client was questioned, it became clear that he was aware of the shock contingency, but not of the fact that his inspection time of "wife slides" had increased.

In the remaining week before his court hearing, the client was allowed home for increasing periods of time, in custody of his wife. She reported that he seemed somewhat depressed, but no more so than before other court appearances in the past. A favourable report about this phase of the treatment was given to the judge, along with the recommendation that Mr. E. be required to return for "booster" treatments when required.

The client was discharged "on trial" at this time, in care of the psychotherapist who had referred him for behavior therapy. He was to return to the hospital for booster shocks, but failed to keep his appointments after the first month, on the grounds that he was doing fine.

He did in fact stay out of trouble for almost two and a half years when a relapse occurred, and he was once again apprehended. At first he did not wish to return to the hospital, but did so when his psychotherapist prevailed upon him to do so.

Apparently he had been free of all desire to exhibit for about a year. After this he suffered some fairly severe reverses in business and in response to the increasing pressure upon him, gradually reverted to his previous habit. He also volunteered the information that he had sought relief from prostitutes, but had again found these contacts unsatisfactory. According to his own statement, he had exhibited many times during the past eighteen months but was caught at it only recently, while exhibiting from his car parked in a shopping center. Although unwilling to receive further shocks, he agreed to having a non-physical form of aversion therapy.

TREATMENT: *Covert Sensitization.*

This method was used in another case described in this book (see Chapter 4). In Mr. E.'s case the preliminary enquiry as to what type of thought content he finds most incompatible with sexual arousal, showed that it was not so much scenes evoking disgust, but those provoking shame or humiliation. The specific fantasy he found most upsetting was one in which he was caught in the act of exhibiting by a member of his immediate family. He was able to write out a particular incident in great detail which had never occurred, but which to him embodied the most devastating experience imaginable. It went briefly as follows:

POSITIVE IMAGE. One day, after having had a particularly unpleasant encounter with an old customer who accused him of overcharging her, he drove away from his store. On the way home he stopped to buy some cigars. The tobacconist's shop was located below street level, and next door to a ladies' hairdresser. He could see the lady nearest the window, sitting under a hairdryer, looking at herself in the mirror. After buying some cigars, he decided to stand outside the hairdresser's and to exhibit, so that the lady under the dryer could see his reflection in the mirror.

NEGATIVE IMAGE. Just as he was doing this, and beginning to masturbate under his open raincoat, someone tapped him on the shoulder. He turned around, and there stood his son, saying, "What are you doing, Dad?"

This theme, and three others like it, were presented to him twice a week for three weeks. It is important that the negative image not be evoked, until the former, positive one has led to some measure of arousal. In cases of this sort, a penile plethysmograph, usually a strain gauge, measuring erectile response, is a helpful device to have. Such equipment not having been available, Mr. E. was asked to signal by a nod when the image of exposing himself to the lady in the mirror was clear in his mind and pleasurable. Then, and only then, was the negative part of the sequence presented.

In our experience, the time taken by the client to signal arousal, following the positive image, increases as treatment progresses. If this does not occur, it is an unfavourable prognostic sign and should lead to a review of the procedure. Perhaps the scene is not optimally arousing, or the client is either unable or unwilling to entertain the image with any degree of clarity. Further training in visualization may be needed in those cases. Failing that, "overt" sensitization (as described in Chapter 4) may be the best alternative.

After six sessions of covert sensitization, the client was very familiar with the procedure. Further repetitions, at this time, would probably have been counterproductive or might even have extinguished the arousal states associated with each theme. The goal now was to make sure that he would use the technique when needed, outside the hospital. For that purpose covert sensitization is superior to physical aversion techniques in that it can be invoked anywhere at any time. To make it even easier for Mr. E. to use the method whenever he felt the need, each theme was tape-recorded for him on a cassette. In this way he could listen to the recording in the privacy of his car, and this he did at irregular intervals.

TREATMENT: *Stress Inoculation.*

Though precise identification of antecedent conditions leading Mr. E. to exhibit, evaded our analysis, his prevailing mood state seemed to be one of the determinants. Most incidents of exhibitionism were ushered in by some disappointment, business problem, or threat affecting his self-esteem. The most recent felony came in the wake of a severe staff problem at work. Also Mr. E. did not conceal the fact that at the time of committing the act, a period of imprisonment would have come as a form of relief. Whatever could be achieved by way of raising his stress tolerance, seemed like a step in the right direction.

Several attempts to manipulate stress tolerance have been published from time to time (Suinn and Richardson, 1971, Gittelman, 1965, Folkins et al., 1968, Bandura et al., 1967), but none seemed as promising as the technique of stress inoculation suggested by Meichenbaum (1972). It consists of teaching the client to emit coping verbalisations in the face of experimentally induced stress. At first it was thought that the specific stressor would have to be the one the client was unable to handle. Later, in Meichenbaum's work, it became apparent that even stressors irrelevant to the client's past experience could be effectively used in stress inoculation.

Mr. E. was therefore encouraged to verbalise coping statements in anticipation of receiving electric shocks at unpredictable intervals. Shock intensity was arbitrarily set at 15 percent above his pain tolerance level, as previously established, and lasted for periods of one second on the average, once every forty-five seconds, (range fifteen to ninety seconds). Between shocks, the client was asked to make verbal statements about his ability to bear these shocks, to say aloud that he would tolerate them without too much physical discomfort, and to express confidence in his ability to stand much higher levels of shock if this were necessary.

At first his verbal statements came haltingly and carried little conviction. After three to four sessions, however, he became more fluent and less stereotyped in his verbal output and was indeed able to stand fairly high shock levels without apparent discomfort. Even allowing for the well-known adaptation effect to continued electric shock, he had surpassed his original tolerance level by 60 percent in eight sessions. He was given this information and considerable social reinforcement for his achievement. Furthermore, he was advised to repeat to himself situation-specific coping statements whenever he found himself anticipating difficult or stressful events.

TREATMENT EVALUATION II:

According to his report, he was able to follow our recommendation with some success, but there can be little doubt that suggestibility contributed to this report to some unknown extent. All one can say at present, is that observations made in this case were consistent with reports by Meichenbaum (1974) and by Ellis (1962) about the modifiability and clinical significance of "what people say to themselves." The work of Watson and Marks (1971) on relevant and irrelevant fear in "flooding" further supports the notion that a stressor used in therapy need not necessarily be relevant to the symptom for treatment to be successful.

DECISION TO TERMINATE TREATMENT:

Following the court hearing, at which Mr. E. was once again sentenced only to a fine, he had three more stress inoculation sessions at his own request. After that it was felt that the recorded sessions of covert sensitization should be sufficient to provide "first aid" should the need arise. He was also urged to return immediately for further shock aversion treatments in the event that his urge to exhibit should recur.

FINAL EVALUATION:

The degree of a client's resistance to deviant behavior, which occurs as infrequently as Mr. E.'s exhibitionism now does, is very difficult to assess. At termination of his second course of behavioral treatment, he claimed that he was once again free of temptation to exhibit and receiving more satisfaction from sex relations with his wife. His wife, however, was not so confident and had in fact become increasingly apprehensive and tense for fear that her husband might suffer yet another relapse. She reported that he had involved himself in all sorts of new enterprises, both at work and at home. Though she was not complaining about this, she did express concern at having to live up to these new commitments, should he be apprehended again. She also felt the strain of his increasing demands on her, socially and sexually.

In view of this unstable marital situation, the couple were advised to continue seeing their psychiatrist, which they did.

FOLLOW-UP:

In the last three years, since termination of the second treatment phase, Mr. E. has reported no adverse incident. He claims to have no desire to exhibit but does experience sexual arousal in the presence of certain women other than his wife. Recently he has had to be hospitalised because of gallbladder trouble. He is doing reasonably well at work and has elaborate plans for the future.

RETROSPECTIVE APPRAISAL:

The case of Mr. E. is fairly representative of results obtained with shock aversion in clients seeking relief from exhibitionism (Feldman, 1966). Given sufficient motivation to complete a course of aversion treatment, it is often possible to eliminate the symptom for a considerable period of time. To consolidate this behavior change, booster treatments are essential and many clients are, naturally, unwilling to submit to these. In this regard much could be achieved by better communication between change agents and law enforcement officers. More recently, some progressive judges have required clients to report for booster treatments as part of parole conditions they imposed.

As this case has shown, there are definite limitations to what physical aversion treatment can achieve. It is, at best, a convenient way of producing a quick suppression of antisocial behavior. Once this has been achieved, other more cognitive techniques are advisable, if the behavior change is to be maintained. Stress inoculation holds some promise in this regard.

TOTAL TIME IN BEHAVIOR THERAPY: *Three and One-half Months.*

REFERENCES

Bandura, A., Grusec, J. E., and Menlove, F. L.: Vicarious extinction of avoidance behavior. *J Pers Soc Psychol, 5*:16-23, 1967.

Ellis, A.: *Reason and Emotion in Psychotherapy.* New York, Lyle Stuart, 1962.

Eysenck, H. J.: *Experiments in Behavior Therapy,* New York, Macmillan, 1967.

Feldman, M. P.: Aversion therapy for sexual deviation. A critical review. *Psychological Bulletin, 65*:65-79, 1966.

Folkins, C. H., Lawson, K. D., Opton, E. M., and Lazarus, R. S.: Desensitization and the experimental reduction of threat. *J Abnorm Psychol, 73*:100-113, 1968.

Gittleman, M.: Behavior rehearsal as a technique in child treatment. *Journal of Child Psychology and Psychiatry, 6*:251-255, 1965.

Meichenbaum, D. H.: Cognitive modification of test-anxious college students. *J Consult Clin Psychol, 39*:370-380, 1972.

Meichenbaum, D. H., and Cameron, R.: The clinical potential of modifying what clients say to themselves. *Psychotherapy: Theory, Research and Practice, 11*:103-107, 1974.

Rachman, S. J., and Teasdale, J.: Aversion Therapy: An appraisal. From C. M. Franks (Eds.): *Behavior Therapy: Appraisal and Status.* New York, McGraw, 1969.

Suinn, R. M., and Richardson, F.: Anxiety management training: A nonspecific behavior therapy program for anxiety control. *Behav Ther, 2*:498-510, 1971.

Watson, J. P., and Marks, I. M.: Relevant and irrelevant fear in flooding: A crossover study of phobic patients. *Behav Ther, 2*:275-293, 1971.

Supplementary Readings

Maletzky, B. M.: "Assisted" covert sensitization in the treatment of exhibitionism. *J Consult Clin Psychol, 42*:34-40, 1974.

Reitz, W. E., and Keil, W. E.: Behavioral treatment of an exhibitionist. *Journal of Behavior Therapy and Experimental Psychiatry, 2*:67-69, 1971.

Rooth, F. G., and Marks, I. M.: Persistent exhibitionism: Short-term response to aversion, self-regulation and relaxation treatments. *Archives of Sexual Behavior, 3*:227-248, 1974.

Wickramasekera, I.: A technique for controlling a certain type of sexual exhibitionism. *Psychotherapy: Theory, Research and Practice, 9*:207-210, 1972.

CHAPTER 8

DIFFERENTIAL SOCIAL REINFORCEMENT

BEHAVIOR PROBLEM: *Inappropriate Personal Habits*
PSYCHIATRIC DIAGNOSIS: *Severe mental retardation (mongoloid)*
MAJOR INTERVENTION: *Differential social reinforcement*
ADDITIONAL METHODS USED: *Contingency management, Aversion therapy, Behavior shaping, Discrimination learning*

General appearance, main complaint and circumstances at intake:

This thirty-year-old male mental defective was referred from another ward in the hospital. Fred had the facial stigmata associated with mongolism and looked considerably younger than his age. He was about five and a half feet tall and appeared to be physically well-developed. Behavior therapy was requested because of a long-standing, socially offensive habit which caused him to be rejected by the other clients and also many staff members. The habit consisted of immersing his head in the toilet bowl while flushing the toilet.

Fred's verbal communication was limited to short, simple sentences often interspersed with inarticulate sounds. He understood some of the things said to him, particularly if he had heard them many times before, such as simple commands, praise, and admonition.

When asked about his "dunking" behavior and why he indulged in it, he responded with a broad grin, shook his head and said: "Fred no dunk."

FAMILY BACKGROUND:

Little is known about Fred's childhood and adolescence. His mother died when he was five. Soon afterwards, the boy was placed in a home for retarded children. The father, who is a construction worker, had not been heard of for many years. Fred is known to have had two younger brothers, neither of whom take any interest in him.

PERSONAL HISTORY:

At the age of twenty, Fred was transferred from the children's home to a psychiatric hospital because of frequent outbursts of aggression aimed at the younger children. He did not like his new environment and was soon victimised by some of the older patients on the ward, who took advantage of his simple-mindedness.

He had previously learned to feed himself and to keep tolerably clean. He now spent most of his time doing repetitive, assembly-type tasks in the industrial workshop and also participated in occupational therapy. He was particularly fond of singing and other musical activities. His attendance in the hospital school was encouraged at first, but soon abandoned because he disturbed the class by striking other patients and using profane language.

His only friend on the ward was a much younger hebephrenic patient with whom he played simple games and occasionally participated in a rhythm band.

In the summer Fred liked to work with the maintenance crew cleaning up the hospital grounds. In the winter he enjoyed snow-shovelling.

HISTORY OF PRESENT PROBLEM:

The bizarre behavior leading to Fred's referral had been first noted five years ago, but had increased in frequency within the last three years. To begin with, he was only reprimanded verbally whenever he emerged from the toilet with dripping hair. When this failed to inhibit the dunking, he was either placed into isolation or occasionally slapped by an attendant. Isolation was imposed by locking him into his room for thirty minutes. Initially, he resisted this, but later requested it on several occasions. At one time, about two years ago, a form of satiation technique was tried. This consisted of forcefully dunking his head in the toilet each time he emerged after a spontaneous dunking.

Eventually the other patients were sensitized to Fred's misdemeanour and reported him to staff whenever they caught him dunking. Socially he became more and more of an outcast on the ward. Even when he had not dunked, no one cared to be in his company.

COMMENT:

Obviously this case presents a behavior disturbing to the patient's social environment, rather than disturbed behavior in the sense of psychopathology. In dealing with such a management problem, the aim is quite different from the usual therapeutic goals in behavior therapy. Instead of helping a client overcome a maladjustment he himself finds undesirable the purpose of intervention here, is to rid the patient of a socially unacceptable habit-pattern thereby making his life in the institution more agreeable. In so doing, one would also hope to produce a greater liking for Fred by those whose daily task it is to care for him. The two events are, of course, reciprocally related in that elimination of the patient's offensive habit would positively affect his social environment, thereby reinstating the natural social reinforcers he had lost as a result of his unacceptable habit.

It is also noteworthy that diligent efforts, over a period of years, to eliminate the dunking through physical punishment and verbal admonition, served only to increase the frequency of dunking. In retrospect there are probably two reasons for this: Physical isolation may not have been perceived as punishment by the patient for whom social deprivation had already become a way of life; and the amount of concern and attention generated by dunking strongly reinforced that operant behavior.

BEHAVIOR ANALYSIS: *Interview*.

All one could ascertain from the limited verbal communication possible with this client was that he lacked all insight into the reason for, and social consequences of his dunking habit.

As far as one could gather from talking to him, he "enjoyed" dunking but could not communicate why plunging his head in the toilet bowl was so pleasurable for him.

Enquiry about the sort of things he found rewarding revealed that he liked food and music. It was not possible to discover through verbal communication what aspect of his environment he experienced as aversive.

BEHAVIOR ANALYSIS: *Observations.*

In general, these observations focused on the antecedents and apparent consequences of spontaneous dunking. Their frequency, duration, and periodicity were also noted.

In the course of one week Fred dunked his head thirty-four times for about two to three minutes on each occasion. The behavior occurred at any time of the day. It was not obviously related to any specific prior behavior of his own, nor was it followed by behavior intended to elicit responses such as anger, punishment or help from staff. When he had dunked, he made no effort to conceal this, but neither did he go out of his way to attract attention to himself. Throughout the observation period, staff were requested to note what they saw, without letting Fred know whether they approved or disapproved.

Occasionally he would display hostile attitudes toward other patients, mainly when they provoked him by teasing or ridicule. If then he was disciplined by staff for being physically aggressive, the likelihood of dunking behavior increased.

BEHAVIOR ANALYSIS: *Test data.*

On the WAIS an I.Q. of 38 was recorded with very little subtest scatter. As expected, the client did somewhat better on performance than on verbal tests. Next, a number of situational tests were carried out to determine what aspect of the dunking sequence seemed to be most reinforcing. It had already been established from observations on the ward, that dunking behavior tended to follow upon some social rebuff or thwarted attempt to act out aggressively. But that did not indicate whether the act of dunking was in itself rewarding, or whether it was indulged in mainly because of the effect it had on the client's social environment. To shed further light on this, some modality-specific effects of Fred's behavior were further investigated.

On the assumption that acoustic effects generated by rushing water in the toilet bowl might be implicated, an attempt was made to simulate that effect by white noise. Hence Fred was provided with white noise stimulation, delivered through earphones, for ten to fifteen minutes every hour to see whether this would reduce his zest for dunking. He visibly enjoyed the white noise sessions, even requested them on occasion, but nevertheless dunked as often as before.

To check out whether the sensation of cold water on his head was maintaining the habit, his head was repeatedly placed under running water in a wash basin. He seemed to be indifferent to this routine. It also had no effect on the frequency of the target behavior. Finally, the smell of some toilet bowls on the ward was changed by spraying them liberally with an ammoniac cleaner. This manoeuvre was also unrewarding; neither frequency nor choice of a dunking site were in the least affected.

COMMENT:

The spectacularly negative outcome of these endeavours led us to conclude that Fred's affinity for dunking was evidently not maintained by modality-specific stimulus seeking. Rather it seemed to be a form of self-stimulation, sometimes ushered in by social rejection. The habit was probably maintained by the extra attention he was getting as a result of it.

TREATMENT GOALS:

(1) Prosocial habit training relevant to self-care.
(2) Manipulation of social reinforcers in client's institutional environment.

TREATMENT STRATEGY:

Not knowing the mode of acquisition underlying Fred's dunking behavior, it seemed appropriate to precede all attempts at unlearning by first teaching him some alternate, pro-social responses relevant to toilet habits. At the same time he was to be socially reinforced whenever he refrained from dunking for a predetermined period. Time-out from such reinforcement was to follow every incident of dunking.

TREATMENT I: *Behavior Shaping and Differential Social Reinforcement.*

These strategies followed immediately upon the observation period. The general procedures are described in Schaefer and Martin (1969). In this particular case Fred was asked to report to staff whenever he wished to use the toilet. He was taken there and given detailed instruction on the appropriate sequence of toilet behaviors from the time he entered the cubicle to the time he washed and dried his hands after leaving it. A member of the staff waited outside the cubicle and provided food reinforcement (generally candy) if Fred emerged without having dunked his head. Going to the wash basin earned him another candy; so did the washing and drying of his hands. Thus, an appropriate toilet behavior sequence was rewarded four times. On occasions when Fred emerged from the cubicle with wet hair, he was scolded for this and no reinforcement was given. Over a period of sixteen days this procedure reduced the average number of daily dunkings from 4.9 in the observation period to .4 per day.

At that time an attempt was made to fade out the food reinforcer and to replace it by social reinforcement for appropriate toilet behavior and "time-out" from social reinforcement when he had dunked. To make sure that this procedure would be followed consistently by all staff members, a yellow "smiley" face was placed on the wall of the nursing station whenever Fred had not dunked for at least three hours. This was a signal for all staff on the ward to go out of their way to praise and encourage his good behavior and to give him extra attention.

Dunking, by contrast, immediately led to replacement of the yellow "smiley" symbol by a red frowning face. This meant that Fred was to be ignored by all staff and preferably confined to an area of the ward where he also had no access to other patients. In the first eight days of that program, average daily dunkings rose to 2.5 and then subsided during the next thirty days to .75 dunkings per day.

By this time it had also become obvious that dunkings were more frequent on days when there were ward meetings. As these were held in a room with a glass door, facing the exit from the toilets, it seemed clear that Fred was still using his same technique to gain attention.

It was therefore decided to introduce shock aversion. Differential social reinforcement alone had apparently accomplished as much as could be expected at this stage.

TREATMENT II: *Shock Aversion.*

The method was essentially that described by Lovaas and his colleagues (Bucher and Lovaas, 1968) for the control of self-destructive behavior in autistic children. A battery-powered, metal rod capable of delivering brief, but painful stimuli to the client's arm or leg, was employed. Again Fred had to notify staff before going to the toilet, and the door was removed from the only cubicle he was permitted to use. As soon as he prepared to dunk his head — but before he actually managed to get his hair wet — a shock was delivered to his upper arm. After the first of these, no further dunking occurred for the next three weeks.

At this point the client developed a severe case of influenza and had to be removed to the infirmary. After his first week there he dunked his head on two occasions. Evidently response generalisation had not occurred. When he returned to the Behavior Therapy Unit four more shocks were administered in the course of the next seventeen days. After that the dunking behavior did not recur for four weeks, not even during ward meetings.

TREATMENT EVALUATION AND DECISION TO TERMINATE:

It was now four months since Fred's admission to behavior therapy, twenty-three days of that period having been spent in the infirmary. There was every indication from his verbal and nonverbal behavior that Fred had learned to discriminate between the significance of the red and yellow signal and that he thoroughly enjoyed the extra attention associated with the yellow face. It was equally clear that occasional appearance of the shock rod, even at a distance, acted as a powerful discriminative stimulus.

Concomitantly, there were some unexpected changes in Fred's aggressive behavior. On admission, a typical behavior sequence began with verbal aggression directed at another patient, followed by hitting or kicking, reproof by staff, and finally dunking; he now mainly expressed aggression by bothering staff before they had a chance to frustrate him. He seemed to have learnt a more direct way of getting the attention he craved.

The problem now was to make sure that the new behavior would generalize to novel situations, different settings and other staff who had not yet become discriminative stimuli for the suppression of dunking behavior. It was felt that this could best be accomplished by acquainting staff on Fred's former ward with the colour signals and by providing them with an inert facsimile of the shock rod to be used as a conditioned aversive stimulus.

FOLLOW-UP:

As is apparent from Figure 4, elimination of Fred's dunking behavior was short-lived. Within a week of transfer to his former environment, he was plunging his head in the toilet almost as often as he had done on admission to behavior therapy.

However, immediate investigation of circumstances surrounding this relapse, revealed its unsuspected cause. Though

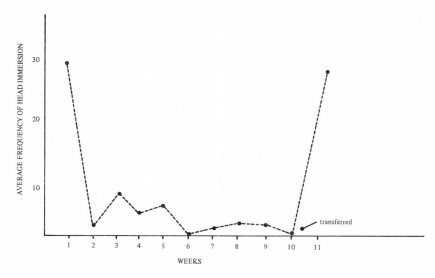

Figure 4. Weekly head immersions by a mental retardate before, during, and after treatment.

the yellow-red signal system for delivery or nondelivery of social reinforcement had been carefully explained to the head nurse on Fred's ward, the message had not reached the night staff nor some nursing staff on other shifts. As a result, the yellow face had remained posted on the nursing station without leading to its intended social consequences. Fred responded quite lawfully to this classical extinction paradigm and reinstated his deviant behavior. The situation was remedied by calling a general meeting of all ward staff to make sure that everyone working there not only knew what to do, but also understood why they were doing it.

Parenthetically, it is worth noting that in large hospital settings such communication problems are not rare and far from easy to resolve. Not only do busy staff members, quite understandably, resent additional routines, but on most hospital wards some personnel may be opposed to the behavioral approach on "ethical" grounds. Unless they can be convinced that the ends justify the means, the program is likely to fail.

(More will be said about these practical issues in the final chapter.)

Four years after termination of treatment, the annual review note states that his dunking habit is no longer a problem, "though it still occurs on occasion, six to eight times a year." Because dunking now occurred so rarely, the signal procedure was discontinued long ago.

That decision may have been premature since the most recent report obtained from a nurse, seven years after treatment, reveals that dunking still occurs "once to twice per night shift." Apparently at that rate the dunking behavior is less bothersome to the staff than reinstatement of the contingency program.

RETROSPECTIVE APPRAISAL:

The therapeutic goals adopted in this case were very different from those envisaged for most other clients described in this book. Even so, the behavioral analysis and the strategies derived from it followed the same pattern as that in most clinical conditioning procedures.

Several months after termination of treatment, some interesting information came to light regarding the probable cause of Fred's unusual habit. It seems that a nurse, who took care of him when he first came to the hospital, used to punish him by sticking his head in the toilet bowl. As was seen earlier, in the context of his response to isolation, Fred had a tendency to seek punishment. Since his dunking behavior was first noted after the punishing nurse had left, it is very probable indeed that she was the source of the behavior.

It is relevant to observe that had this aspect of Fred's reinforcement history been known before his admission to our unit, it might have simplified the behavioral analysis, but would probably not have affected the remedial strategy to which it led. As such, this case illustrates the familiar claim of many behavior therapists, that knowing the cause of a disorder is not necessarily helpful in selecting the most effective technique for its alleviation.

TOTAL TIME IN BEHAVIOR THERAPY: *Four months.*

REFERENCES

Bucher, B., and Lovaas, O. I.: Use of aversive stimulation in behavior modification. In M. R. Jones (Ed.): *Miami Symposium on the Prediction of Behavior*, 1967. Aversive stimulation. Miami, U of Miami Pr, 1968.

Schaefer, H. H., and Martin, P. L.: *Behavior Therapy.* New York, McGraw, 1969.

Supplementary Readings

Gelfand, D. M., Gelfand, S., and Dobson, W. R.: Unprogrammed reinforcement of patients' behavior in a mental hospital. *Behav Res Ther,* 5:201-207, 1967.

Hagen, R. L., Craighead, W. E. and Paul, G. L.: Staff reactivity to evaluative behavioral observations. *Behav Ther,* 6: 1975.

Kazdin, A. E.: Response cost: The removal of conditioned reinforcers for therapeutic change. *Annual Review of Behavior Therapy: Therapy and Practice.* 2:173-186, 1974.

Lovibond, S. H.: Aversive control of behavior. *Behav Ther.* 1:80-91, 1970.

Sidman, H.: Operant techniques. In G. J. Bachrach (Ed.): *Experimental Foundations of Clinical Psychology.* New York, Basic, 1962.

PART FOUR: DISCUSSION

CHAPTER 9

SOME CURRENT PROBLEMS IN APPLIED BEHAVIOR MODIFICATION

T HE final chapter raises issues which generally impede the clinical application of conditioning techniques. Some of these have been discussed elsewhere, but summarising them in one chapter may contribute to a fuller understanding of their interrelatedness. The subject matter will be presented in dischotomous form. This is done in the interest of brevity and to polarize the issues concerned. In practise, of course, they are more often present as continuing dialogues reflecting conflicts of interest or divergent theoretical positions.

THE MEDICAL vs. THE BEHAVIORAL MODEL

Nowhere has the straitjacket of either/or formulations been more stultifying than in the rivalry between conceptual models of behavior pathology and behavior change. Ever since the advent of behavior modification in the late 1950s its practitioners have insisted that successful behavior change does not depend on prior understanding of factors causing maladaptive behavior. Others have gone further and argued that even when the cause is known, such knowledge is not necessarily relevant to treatment or prognosis (Eysenck, 1960). The case of Fred (described in Chapter 8) illustrates this point.

But this is not to say that the relationship between symptom and cause in the behavior disorders is necessarily different from that seen in some physical disorders. It merely implies that maladaptive behavior, often acquired through faulty learning, may be amenable to elimination by some form of new learning, relearning, or unlearning. This may be true even in cases where nonbehavioral factors such as "inner conflicts" or "family dynamics" contributed to symptom formation.

In the past it was often argued that removal of symptoms alone would lead to symptom substitution. When this turned out not to be the case, opponents of behavior modification sometimes contended that the results of conditioning techniques would be short-lived. In addition, it was claimed that behavioral methods fail to deal with subjective elements of the client's complaint and, therefore, represent a mechanistic and "dehumanized" approach to psychological distress.

To battle arguments on either side of this controversy surely amounts to an exercise in futility. Only if the medical and behavioral models were indeed mutually exclusive would there be need for careful evaluation of their relative merits. Fortunately this is not the case. To anyone familiar with the multiplicity of problems seen in most psychiatric settings, it is patently clear that some cases are amenable to behavior analysis, and others are dealt with more effectively in terms appropriate to the medical model. In many instances both approaches are appropriate, often leading to two treatment strategies, each derived from a different model. Also it is sometimes overlooked that there are alternatives to both the behavioral and the medical model in treating deviant behavior. Rational Emotive Therapy, Remotivation and Industrial Therapy are cases in point.

Perhaps the crucial distinction between medical and behavioral models, relevant to this book, lies in the role they assign to environmental factors in the causation of behavior disorders. If learning theorists are correct in believing that much disordered behavior is under external stimulus control, then manipulation of the client's environment rightly becomes an integral part of any treatment program.

Considerations of this kind have definite ramifications for the formulation of therapeutic goals. One example emerging from the case histories cited in this volume arises from the distinction between "behavioral problem" and "psychiatric diagnosis." Indeed, the difference between treating an "irrational avoidance response" rather than an "obsessive compulsive neurosis"; or "maladaptive verbal behavior" rather than a "hysterical reaction" is more than a play on words. It reflects not only a semantic distinction but also a host of assumptions about the nature of symptoms, the role of the therapist and the choice of intervention. These factors, in turn, determine the expected outcome of therapy and its evaluation.

Yet, to espouse a particular theoretical position need not imply intolerance of alternate orientations. So far, no single approach to the treatment of deviant behavior has shown itself so superior to all other techniques that it should rightfully dominate the field. Nor is this likely to happen, in view of the multiplicity of factors known to contribute to behavior pathology and its complex manifestations.

The case studies presented in this book were intended to illustrate a behavioral orientation to various stages of clinical problem-solving. One salient aspect of this approach concerns the role of the therapist. It deserves special comment, as it is often the point on which proponents of rival treatment models disagree. The doctor-patient relationship is a unique phenomenon, at least in western society, and many psychotherapists attribute to it a major role in determining therapeutic outcome. Not so behavior therapists, who tend to discount its importance and prefer to link behavior change directly to what is learned in the course of a behavioral intervention. Oddly enough the learning experience which results from a client interacting with a change agent is often overlooked. For this reason it will be more fully explored below.

For convenience, and to highlight the points at issue, the traditional "doctor-patient" relationship will be contrasted with that of change agent and client.* For each dimension of interaction the role preference of the helper will be contrasted with the role expectations he has of the help seeker. Five important aspects of clinical interaction as listed in Table I will be considered, i.e. background, locus of intervention, vehicle of change, therapeutic strategy, and decision making. Inevitably, descriptive tabulations, in bipolar form, sometimes suggest clear cut dichotomies where, in fact, only continuous grada-

---

*The term "doctor" in this context could stand for psychotherapist, semantic therapist, or any other person who sees the nature of his relationship to the help seeker as a necessary condition of therapeutic change.

TABLE I

Comparison of the Medical and Behavioral Model
In Terms of Dyadic Interaction Patterns

Dimension of Interaction	MEDICAL		BEHAVIORAL	
	Doctors' role preference	Doctors' expectation of patient	Change agents' role preference	Change agents' expectation of client
a. *BACKGROUND* Professional – nonprofessional	Professional	Nonprofessional	Often nonprofessional	Nonprofessional
b. *LOCUS OF INTERVENTION* Stationary – mobile	Stationary	Mobile	Mobile	Mobile
c. *VEHICLE OF CHANGE* Verbal – nonverbal	Verbal	Verbal and nonverbal	Verbal and nonverbal	Verbal and nonverbal
d. *THERAPEUTIC STRATEGY* Initiates – accepts	Initiates	Accepts	Initiates	Initiates
e. *DECISION MAKING* Singly – jointly	Singly	Jointly	Jointly	Jointly

tions of dimensional differences are found. With that hazard in mind, the following additional specifications are offered.

Background

PROFESSIONAL-NONPROFESSIONAL: By definition, the doctor-patient relationship involves at least one professionally trained person. On the other hand, use of nonprofessional personnel as change agents, (for instance parents, spouses, etc.) is greatly on the increase. Help seekers, whether patients or clients, are mostly nonprofessional.

Locus of Intervention

STATIONARY-MOBILE: Traditional therapies in psychiatric settings are generally dispensed in an office or institution. Despite the recent proliferation of community psychiatric clinics the psychotherapist rarely goes into the patient's home, much less into his work, school, or community setting. In behavior modification the opposite is often true. Not only is the therapeutic intervention frequently carried out *in vivo,* but significant persons in the client's environment are recruited as "allies in reinforcement." Particularly teachers, parents, relatives, or friends are involved in this way, especially toward the end of many treatment programs. Consequently, the change agent may be required to perform his duties remote from his office or the clinic. This enables him to judge the client's progress, not only in the course of formal treatment sessions, but also in extra-therapeutic situations where the need for behavior change originally arose.

Vehicle of Change

VERBAL-NONVERBAL: Though verbal communication is an important aspect of all therapeutic interventions, it is the major vehicle of the psychotherapies. Adherents of the behavioral model additionally use many other procedures in which the motor or autonomic behavior of the client becomes the focus of attention and often determines therapeutic strategy and outcome.

Therapeutic Strategy

INITIATES-ACCEPTS: Whereas both psychotherapists and change agents may be active in the therapeutic role, patients often see themselves as passive recipients of somatic, drug, and psychotherapies. Thus one "receives" electroconvulsive shock, or medication, and "is in" psychotherapy, whereas clients seeking behavior therapy are encouraged to involve themselves in the relearning process. Hence they are said to be "doing" relaxation or "taking part" in behavior rehearsal, assertive training, or desensitization *in vivo*. The client is made to realize, from the start, that the outcome of his behavioral treatment depends to some large extent on his personal effort. To that end he is expected to carry out homework assignments and occasionally to provide the therapist with behavioral data collected between visits.

Decision Making

SINGLY-JOINTLY: In all forms of treatment the therapist is ultimately responsible, and final decisions as to what form therapy should take must therefore rest with him. But in the process of arriving at decisions regarding what method of behavior therapy to use, how fast and intensively to apply it and when to terminate treatment, the client generally has a say. Procedures derived from the medical model more often tend to be imposed upon the patient by unilateral decision of the therapist. In medical practice this is frequently well-justified because patients cannot be expected to judge the relative merits of highly specialized treatment alternatives, especially if these are presented in esoteric terminology. Hence patients learn to believe that "doctor knows best" and expect to be told what to do.

Whether a similar attitude to psychotherapy is appropriate is debatable. Where it does exist, the tendency is for the doctor to make most major decisions. All the patient actually decides is whether to stay in therapy. Once he has opted to continue treatment, he rarely participates in further decision making. In some instances, particularly with children or court cases, treatment may even be carried out against the patient's wishes.

If this analysis of dyadic interaction patterns accurately reflects at least the dominant trends differentiating adherents of the behavioral and medical model, then two consequences emerge. First, inspection of Table I reveals that each of the five dimensions of interaction lead to role-expectation patterns concordant for change agent and client, but discordant in the doctor-patient relationship. Assuming that the behavior modelled by therapists during treatment exercises some influence on those he treats, one would expect the effect of observational learning to be greater in concordant dyadic relationships.

A second point, directly related to the first, is that learning of interpersonal strategies, such as occur in therapeutic relationships, might be expected to contribute to symptom alleviation, at least in some disorders. A learning process of this kind has long been postulated by dynamic theorists, yet the author knows of no systematic study attempting to assess the effect of interpersonal learning on treatment outcome. The work of Truax and Mitchell (1971) on the necessary and sufficient conditions of therapeutic change, and Bandura's (1969) studies on the determinants of social learning through modelling techniques come closest to dealing with these variables. So far, however, no one seems to have related the possible effect of dyadic interaction patterns on treatment outcome. Until this is done one can only side with those critics of behavior modification who point out that ignoring the quality of a helping relationship does not make that variable irrelevant to what is achieved in behavior therapy.

PRACTICE vs. RESEARCH

The eight case-studies presented in this book clearly illustrate the gulf that still exists between clinical applications of conditioning techniques and the research findings from which they stem. There is nothing unusual about this; it is a well-known phenomenon in most branches of applied science. In the behavioral sciences it is particularly bothersome, because so much of the basic research on learning was done on infrahuman species and cannot, therefore, directly inform the clinician. What is needed, as an intermediate step, are studies of a comparative nature, and these are still quite rare. They also tend to be inconclusive for clinical purposes, unless they are done in the context of naturally-occurring or experimentally-induced behavior pathology.

Flooding techniques, as described in Chapter 2, are a good example. Theoretically, they are based on the well-established

process of experimental extinction, resulting from nonreinforcement of a conditioned response. Clinically, the uncondi-
tioned response in question, is autonomic arousal (anxiety)
elicited by a once neutral, or at least harmless, stimulus. Escape
from or avoidance of that stimulus leads to reduced arousal,
which is generally taken to be the reinforcing event favouring
maintenance of the maladaptive avoidance or escape response.

Extinction theory would predict that deliberate exposure of
an organism to the feared stimulus, and prevention of the escape response, would in time, also lead to reduced arousal. At
that point, increased "stimulus tolerance" is presumably also
rewarded by tension reduction. Since the organism now has a
chance to learn that the conditioned stimulus does not lead to
an aversive arousal state, the instrumental avoidance response
(phobic reaction) is diminished.

Similar predictions from learning theory, promising though
they are, do not offer the clinician much guidance for implementation of therapeutic procedures. How long should the
client be exposed to the aversive stimulus; with what intensity;
alone or in company of the therapist? Also, how should the
client be prepared for the session and instructed during it?

Thanks to some innovative animal experimentation, mainly
by Baum (1970) a few of the crucial variables enumerated above
were explored in rats with experimentally induced avoidance
responses. Thus it was possible to infer that the flooding process in humans would probably be enhanced by prolonged
exposure to the aversive stimulus, the client being engaged in
some distracting task, while in the company of the therapist.
Though necessarily speculative, this sort of link between laboratory and clinic is unfortunately still the exception rather than
the rule. Some of the difficulties inherent in extrapolating from
animal studies to clinical applications of flooding have been
detailed by Baum and Poser (1971).

What is particularly significant about the comparative approach is that it is not based on a one-way flow of information.
The fact that Mrs. R. (described in Chapter 2) did not show the
human equivalent of "freezing," that she made no attempt to
escape from the situation, and that only the compulsive, but

not the obsessive, element of her symptoms was alleviated by flooding were not predictable consequences of this treatment. These observations should be at least as challenging to the researcher as the researcher's data were to the clinician. Regrettably, that is rarely the case, probably because researchers and practitioners still tend to operate in two solitudes. This "isolationist" situation persists despite valiant efforts over twenty-five years to implement the scientist-professional model of clinical psychology (Raimy, 1950).

Yet another barrier to closer cooperation between data-producers and data-consumers is the conflict of commitment one encounters between those whose allegiance is to the healing arts as against those committed to the behavioral sciences (Loevinger, 1963). Basically, institutions dedicated to the delivery of mental health care, find themselves at odds with the demands on space, time, and equipment commonly made by researchers. This is understandable since researchers and clinicians subscribe to different value systems, determined by differences in their respective sources of reinforcement. Clinicians are typically rewarded for having large case loads, limited staff, high patient turnover, and low readmission rates; whereas researchers are invested in elegant (and sometimes costly) research designs, data acquisition, quantitative evaluation of results, and publication. It has thus far been difficult for most training institutions to reconcile these aims, partly because role models in academic psychology departments tend to be researchers first, while those in medical schools are primarily practising clinicians. Nothing short of a joint training program for psychologically trained behavior change agents and medically trained clinicians is likely to resolve that impasse.

Arising from the conflict of commitment is the troublesome matter of trying to meet scientific criteria in clinical practise. Though it is a fundamental tenet of all scientific enquiry not to manipulate more than one variable at a time, this is patently impossible in most clinical settings. As illustrated by the case-studies in this book, clients usually participate in two or three interventions sometimes consecutively but often concurrently. This makes it very difficult to ascribe outcome of therapy to a specific intervention. Instead, the clinical investigator has to content himself with establishing covariance between delivery of a composite "treatment package" and subsequent behavior change.

Not only does the clinical practitioner have to accommodate to this limitation, but the clinical researcher does as well, though to a lesser degree. Even in well-controlled studies with human subjects, experimenter-effects on the outcome of a particular procedure can hardly ever be fully assessed, let alone eliminated. Recent attempts at automation of therapy (Lang et al., 1970; Donner and Guerny, 1969) may offer solutions to this problem, but even then, the way clients are prepared, instructed, and motivated to continue automated therapy must have some bearing on the results achieved. Recognising the role of therapist variables as one determinant of therapeutic outcome need not, however, invite research nihilism or the equally false conclusion that only the personality of the therapist counts. Our clients were typically treated by more than one therapist to give them a chance to practice their newly-acquired response repertoires in different social situations. In this way their response to reinforcement contingencies operating outside the hospital was hopefully facilitated. Evidently not all change agents are equally therapeutic for all clients, but nor are the people clients meet in everyday life. In essence, this is one way of building generalisation into the therapeutic process. Failure to do so may partially account for the high rate of readmission or relapse following exclusively dyadic treatment models.

Mention should also be made of the hardware required for behavior modification. Many clinicians are prepared to try behavioral techniques, but are put off, or even frightened by the impressive apparatus seen in some behavioral research departments. The following three objections are frequently voiced: Behavior therapy is too expensive; many therapists lack the "engineering" skills to operate and maintain the equipment; and instrumentation is "dehumanizing" and causes the client "apparatus stress." The first two objections are sometimes justified, but they are rarely insuperable. The third might be unfounded in view of the increased prevalence of "prosthetic devices" encountered in most walks of life by almost everyone, in and out of hospitals. But in the main, it has been our experience that for most forms of behavior therapy, very little equipment is needed, provided that sufficient staff is available. Only in understaffed settings with many clients does the use of programming equipment and automation become a necessity. The skills required to operate most standard equipment can be acquired in the course of a brief in-service training period.

CLINICAL vs. ACTUARIAL ASSESSMENT

Problems under this heading follow directly from our discussion of the previous issue.

In the late 1950s and early 1960s when the application of behavior therapy to a wide variety of clinical cases was first reported, single case studies were the order of the day. While the process of intervention was fully described in those cases, information about outcome was often sketchy and almost invariably based on the therapist's own clinical observations (Ullmann & Krasner, 1965). Follow-up was of necessity brief or nonexistent.

Later, particularly after the widespread introduction of standardized behavior tests (Lang and Lazovik, 1963, Lovibond, 1964, and Paul, 1968) and reversal and multiple baseline techniques (Baer et al., 1968), there followed a period of greater insistence on rigorous evaluation of therapeutic outcome.

For reasons outlined above, this trend toward greater objectivity in the assessment of treatment results was slow to spread beyond the confines of research publications into behavior therapy service settings.

Even though behavior modification owes its original impact to its roots in learning theory and experimentation which promised a more objective approach to therapy than was hitherto available, that promise was not always fulfilled. As more and more busy practitioners in the mental health field integrated conditioning methods into their professional armamentarium, the extra time required to establish pretherapy baselines and measures of behavior change often caused these quantitative, assessment techniques to be dropped. In their place less time-consuming and more familiar clinical evaluations were reintroduced. In many instances this meant a return to the simple but highly unreliable categorization of clients into those who were unchanged, slightly improved, much improved or cured. What is worse, these judgments were frequently made by the patient's own therapist, thereby introducing additional distortion in the direction of "false positives."

Even questionnaires and rating scales, frequently resorted to in case material presented in this book, are second best. While they save time in getting certain items of information and introduce at least some degree of objectivity, they basically remain to be self-report techniques, with all the weaknesses inherent in that data base.

Though often cumbersome, there is much to be gained from obtaining systematic behavior ratings on clients from their relatives or friends. Where this is impractical, home visits by a social worker or other observer not directly involved in the treatment process can be very helpful in getting more objective feedback than self-ratings provide.

Ultimately, there is no substitute for an *in vivo* behavior sample reflecting changes in the target behavior being treated. Only in this way is it possible to obtain outcome data on a wide variety of cases, in terms amenable to verification by others than client or therapist. Such data need not become so atomistic as to lose in relevance what they gain in objectivity. Ideally, before the beginning of treatment every therapist should be able to make explicit just what parameters of the target behavior are expected to change, in terms of what test procedure and as a result of which intervention.

Disclosure by the change agent of his specific treatment goals, prior to intervention, is a necessary prerequisite for such a procedure as is the establishment of baselines. Of necessity this requires that treatment be withheld during an initial observation period. The objection that this is too costly or time consuming is hard to maintain in view of the blind alleys evaded and false starts avoided by this procedure.

The clinical vs. actuarial debate also touches on case selection. At present this is almost entirely done on the basis of practical considerations and the hunches of individual clinicians. In the absence of valid prognostic devices it could hardly be otherwise. But it would be useful to have instruments capable of distinguishing those clients likely to respond to behavior therapy from those not likely to do so.

The usual techniques of clinical assessment, conceived as they were in the context of psychodynamic theory, are not adequate predictors of behavior therapeutic outcome, hardly surprising when one considers the differences in therapeutic aims known to be associated with various treatment methods. None of them has thus far succeeded in elaborating adequate predictors of clients' responses to therapy.

In all probability tests measuring, as directly as possible, a person's susceptibility to autonomic, verbal, and skeletal conditioning, will in the long run, provide better indices of behavior therapeutic outcome than do diagnostic instruments based, as they mostly are, on pencil-and-paper self reports.

RESIDENTIAL vs. OUTPATIENT CARE

The eight cases discussed in this volume were all confined to hospital during the course of their treatment. Even so, observations of their behavior were often carried out in other settings. In some instances, particularly during the rehabilitation phase, further treatments were given in the client's home or place of work.

By the criteria of client accessibility and environmental control, residential treatment has obvious advantages over seeing clients only sporadically during out-patient visits. Certain cases, such as those described in Chapters 1, 2, 3, 6, 7, and 8 could, by nature of their impairment, not have been dealt with outside a hospital; others like Mr. A. (Chapter 4) or Mrs. S. (Chapter 5) probably could have. What are the relative merits of these alternative treatment settings?

Clearly residential treatment affords the change agent greater control over treatment programs than he would otherwise have.

Where the target problem calls for rigid operant control of a client's daily activities there may be no alternative to an in-service program or even a closed treatment facility.

Within a hospital unit it is also easier to provide a wider range of auxiliary services such as occupational therapy, supervised work areas, and of course, physical care. Furthermore, continuity of observation is much enhanced and the opportunity to see how clients structure their leisure time and the opportunity to monitor their nocturnal activities may be helpful in certain cases.

But in-service management also has some disadvantages. It involves behavior therapists in a great deal of responsibility and decision making only tangentially related to their area of expertise. Mealtimes have to be supervised, occupational and recreational activities planned, visitors and weekend leaves coordinated, not to mention the need for day and night staff as well as the provision of general health care. All of this makes residential care for behavior therapy somewhat costly, particularly in view of the relatively large staff required for even modest case loads. Where a residential treatment unit also serves as a teaching facility, restrictions on the range of available case material may be an additional drawback.

Clients suitable for outpatient care naturally tend to be less impaired, less chronic, and more mobile; for these reasons they are generally amenable to a wider range of interventions than are resident cases. On the other hand, their treatment programs are far more difficult to control and the assessment of change and outcome is correspondingly less reliable. Continuity of treatment, so essential to successful conduct of most conditioning therapies, is often hard or impossible to bring about. Also, it is not uncommon for clients to undo, in their extra-therapeutic activities, whatever small gains were achieved in the early phases of treatment. This necessarily prolongs the recovery period, sometimes needlessly.

On the positive side, the type of clients mostly referred to outpatient clinics show quicker and more complete response to treatment than do inpatients. This is reinforcing for staff whose motivation is thereby maintained at a higher level. The wide variety of problems referred creates greater challenge and provides a rich source of suitable teaching material. Last but not least, such an enterprise is more economically run and less wasteful of highly-trained staff by virtue of the fact that all of their time is spent on the implementation of behavioral strategies.

Location of the behavioral treatment center is yet another consideration. If it is housed in a private institute or consulting practice, residential care in most cases is precluded on financial grounds. Conversely, a behavior therapy service attached to a mental hospital is generally called upon to treat residential clients. In such settings it may be difficult to treat nonresidents because they are often reluctant to attend hospitals they associate with long-term mental illness.

The optimal location for a behavior therapy service seems to be a general hospital with facilities for both types of care. Clients can then be assigned to whichever program best meets their needs. As these needs may change in the course of therapy, the flexibility such a hospital affords is a distinct advantage.

PROFESSIONAL vs PARAPROFESSIONAL TRAINING

This is still a controversial issue in many clinical service settings, whatever their theoretical orientation. Although the effectiveness of nonprofessional workers has been demonstrated in controlled studies, both in individual psychotherapy (Rioch et al., 1963) and group therapy (Poser, 1966), no comparable data exists for behavior therapy as yet. This is not surprising since specialized training in applied behavior therapy is of very recent origin.

Whereas practically every major psychology department in North American universities now offers courses in behavior modification, there is still a critical shortage of clinical settings offering supervised training in a wide range of behavior therapy methods applicable to varied case material. Hence, one is forced to conclude that most contemporary practitioners of behavior therapy are self-taught. Only in the mid 1960s did a few centers in Britain and the United States begin to offer more or less formal training programs in behavior therapy. As a rule these were available only to qualified psychologists and medical practitioners.

Even now only a few behavior therapy settings recognize two levels of training for potential change agents, where one is intended for behavior therapy assistants and the other prepares mental health professionals for senior positions as behavior therapists (Poser, 1967, Poser & Ashem, 1968). Those at Level I, who have little or no background in clinical psychology or learning theory, are trained as observers and cotherapists for procedures such as relaxation, modeling, behavior rehearsal, and contingency management. Those with previous clinical training and experience are likewise expected to achieve competence at Level I and also to acquire familiarity with the behavioral literature. Subsequently, they are "apprenticed" to senior therapists until they demonstrate competence to conduct their own intake interviews and to implement treatment strategies under minimal supervision. By means of such training programs a fair number of professional and paraprofessional staff could be made available to provide behavioral treatment services.

The two-level concept of training behavior therapists still seems appropriate, if only to alleviate the enduring manpower shortage of treatment personnel. If behavior therapy is to have the impact it deserves, it must capitalize on the fact that many of its techniques can be routinized, if not automated. But to do this competently, technicians are required to make these procedures available on a large scale. Advanced professional training is required only of those who are to determine therapeutic strategies, develop new ones, or otherwise participate in clinical decision making.

It should also be recognized that the training of personnel at two levels simultaneously presents some problems in communication, and hence in efficiency of the training procedure. Because of this it may be preferable to conduct two independent training programs, one for the professionally qualified and another for behavior therapy technicians.

The argument that paraprofessional personnel tend to overreach themselves, or lack judgement in crisis situations, has received no support from our experience. At the same time nonprofessional workers should not be encouraged to do behavior therapy in the absence of trained supervisors.

A more substantive objection to the large-scale output of behavior therapy technicians arises from their lack of occupational identity. This is a serious problem affecting paraprofessionals in all disciplines. As such, its consideration lies beyond the scope of this book.

SHORT-TERM vs. LONG-TERM OUTCOME

No account of current problems in applied behavior modification would be complete without reference to the need for long-term outcome studies. Few of these have appeared thus far, partly because the widespread clinical application of behavior therapy is scarcely ten years old. Also there are vast obstacles to the collection of meaningful follow-up data. Chief among these are

(1) The mobility of patients over time.
(2) The confounding effect of intercurrent therapeutic experiences, formal or casual.
(3) The occurrence of life crises, or their fortuitous absence, at the time of evaluation.
(4) Client bias in favour of reporting recovery.
(5) Maturational change.

All of these are variables not easily controlled in the clinical assessment of therapeutic change. Also, there are still unresolved methodological issues including:

(6) How to measure change (i.e. the criterion problem)?
(7) What constitutes an appropriate control for spontaneous recovery?
(8) Who is the appropriate informant (i.e. the client, significant others, law enforcement agencies, etc.)?
(9) Who should gather the information (the therapist, his colleagues, or research technicians unfamiliar with the clients and the therapy being evaluated)?

(10) Statistical inference (e.g. the problem of initial value and change)?

In view of these difficulties, it is easy to understand why so few long-term, follow-up studies have appeared.

That short-term outcome data can be very misleading was amply illustrated by the eight cases presented in this book. In their therapists' view all but one of these, were distinctly improved at termination of treatment. Yet by the time of their most recent follow-up, five to ten years after discharge, only two gave clear evidence of having completely overcome the target symptom for which they were originally treated. Of the other six, four are definitely improved by the criterion of showing sufficient control of their symptoms to be able to function to their own satisfaction and that of their immediate family. One, who managed extremely well for seven years after treatment, relapsed just before the final follow-up and the remaining client is still hospitalised and unimproved by behavior therapy.

As stated at the outset, clients described in this book were not randomly selected. Even so, their problems are fairly representative of the type of disorder behavior therapists are likely to encounter in residential treatment centers affiliated with large psychiatric institutions. It is therefore of interest to summarize briefly some actuarial data pertaining to this subsample of eight clients and to review at least some of their responses to the follow-up questionnaire (see Appendix for reference to the questions asked).

SEVERITY OF DYSFUNCTION: Conservatively estimated, the target symptoms treated in this group had a median duration of seven years with a range from four to twenty years. As such, most of them were well beyond the five year period in which 90 percent of neurotic patients are sometimes said to overcome their symptoms "spontaneously" (Eysenck, 1952). Also two of them were clearly psychotic and one was severely retarded, making it even less likely that such changes as were effected in this sample, came about fortuitously.

LENGTH OF TREATMENT: Perhaps because of the long-standing target problems in these cases, behavior therapy did not emerge as a particularly rapid intervention. The median hospital stay in behavior therapy for this group was eight months (range 3.5 to 24 months). Nearly all of them had, however, been treated before by other forms of therapy outside hospital for at least three years and some of the group for much longer than that.

With these facts in mind, the clients' responses to the follow-up interview are quite informative. Their answers to question 4 reveals that six out of eight have not sought treatment for the target problem dealt with in behavior therapy since they left hospital, and none of them felt that another symptom had taken its place (question 5). Three of them were still on medication at the final follow-up, but all three had been on similar drugs prior to behavior therapy (question 7). Six out of eight were working (question 8), and seven rated their social (or marital) adjustment as improved (question 9). By comparison to the way they felt when admitted for Behavior Therapy seven out of eight claimed to be "much better" (question 12).

It is also noteworthy that despite the use of aversive interventions such as flooding, covert sensitization, and faradic stimulation, five out of eight said they would choose behavior therapy in preference to other interventions were they to require mental health care in the future. The remaining three were undecided or unable to judge, (question 10). One of those (who had received, and benefited from Flooding therapy, see Chapter 2) found the treatment "terrible." All others rated the therapeutic interventions they received as either "not unpleasant" or "indifferent" (question 11).

Wherever possible, information received from clients was checked out with at least one other observer and the follow-up interviews were conducted by assistants not previously known to the patients. Despite these precautions, the size and selection of our sample permit no valid inference regarding the outcome of Behavior Therapy, even with similar clients seen elsewhere. At best it was shown that for most cases described in this volume, behavioral interventions had an ameliorative effect clearly discernible five to ten years after termination of treatment.

REFERENCES

Baer, D., Wolf, M. M., and Risley, T. R.: Some current dimensions of applied behavior analysis. *Journal of Applied Behavior Analysis, 1*:91-97, 1968.

Bandura, A.: *Principles of Behavior Modification,* New York, HR&W, 1969.

Baum, M.: Extinction of avoidance responding through response prevention (flooding). *Psychological Bulletin, 74*:276-284, 1970.

Baum, M., and Poser, E. G.: Comparison of flooding procedures in animals and man. *Behav Res Ther, 9*:249-254, 1971.

Donner, L., and Guerny, G. G., Jr.: Automated group desensitization for test anxiety. *Behav Res Ther, 7*:1-13, 1969.

Eysenck, H. J.: *Behavior Therapy and the Neuroses.* London, Pergamon Press, 1960.

Eysenck, H. J.: The effects of psychotherapy: an evaluation. *J Consult Clin Psychol, 16*:319-324, 1952.

Lang, P. J., and Lazovik, A. D.: Experimental desensitization of a phobia. *J Abnorm Soc Psychol, 66*:519-525, 1963.

Lang, P. J., Melamed, B. G., and Hart, J.: A psychophysiological analysis of fear modification using an automated desensitization procedure. *J Abnorm Psychol, 76*:220-234, 1970.

Loevinger, J.: The conflict of commitment in clinical research, *American Psychologist, 18*:241-251, 1963.

Lovibond, S. H.: *Conditioning and enuresis.* Oxford, Pergamon, 1964.

Paul, G. L.: *Insight Versus Desensitization in Psychotherapy: An Experiment in Anxiety Reduction.* Stanford, Stanford U Pr, 1968.

Poser, E. G.: The effect of therapist's training on group therapeutic outcome. *J Consult Clin Psychol, 30*:283-289, 1966.

Poser, E. G.: Training behavior therapists. *Behav Res Ther, 5*:37-41, 1967.

Poser, E. G.: The teaching of behavior modification in an interdisciplinary setting. In R. D. Rubin and C. M. Franks: *Advances in Behavior Therapy 1968.* New York, Academic Press, 1969.

Raimy, V. (Ed.): *Training in Clinical Psychology,* Englewood Cliffs, P-H, 1950.

Rioch, M. J., Elkes, E., Flint, A. A., Usdansky, B. C., Newman, R. G., and Silber, E.: National Institute of Mental Health pilot study in training mental health counselors. *Am J Orthopsychiatry, 33*:678-689, 1963.

Truax, C. B., and Mitchell, K. M.: Research on certain therapist interpersonal skills and relation to process and outcome. In Bergin and Garfield (Eds.): *Handbook of Psychotherapy and Behavior Change: An Empirical Analysis.* New York, Wiley, 1971.

Ullmann, L. P., and Krasner, L.; *Case Studies in Behavior Modification,* New York, HR&W, 1965.

APPENDIX
Follow-up Inquiry

NAME: _____   Date of Discharge
From B.T.U.

ADDRESS: _____   _____

DATE: _____

TELEPHONE NO: _____

(1) What kind of complaint led you to seek treatment or be referred to Behavior Therapy?
(Please be specific). _____
_____

(2) Is the above complaint still bothering you? If yes, please describe how often and with what intensity.
_____
_____

(3) If your original complaint is no longer bothering you, when did it disappear?
    a. At termination of treatment _____
    b. Some weeks later _____
    c. Some months later _____
    d. Does it come and go _____

(4) Since the end of your treatment here have you sought treatment anywhere else for this complaint? If so, with what results?
_____
_____

(5) If your complaint is no longer in evidence do you feel that some other problem has taken its place?
_____
_____

163

(6) If you still have a residual complaint, how do you rate your chances of overcoming your problem completely?

_____

_____

(7) Since leaving here have you been on any medication? Are you on medication now?

_____

_____

(8) Are you now working? If so, where?

_____

_____

(9) Is your social (marital) life satisfactory?

_____

_____

(10) If you required further help for your original complaint or any other behavior disorder, would you choose the same treatment, i.e. behavior therapy, in preference to some other form of mental health care?

_____

_____

(11) Did you find your treatment by behavior therapy pleasant or unpleasant?

_____

_____

(12) You originally came to this Unit _____
By comparison to the way you felt at that time, do you now feel
Much the same as at a little better ____ worse ____
admission _____ much better _____

(13) Additional Remarks:

_____

_____

AUTHOR INDEX

A

Agras, S., 35
Alexander, F., xv, xxv
Ascough, J. C., 92
Ashem, B., 158, 162
Ayllon, T., 46, 53
Azrin, N. H., 46, 53

B

Bachrach, G. J., 139
Baer, D., 86, 91, 153, 162
Bandura, A., xviii, xxvi, 124, 127, 149, 162
Barlow, D., 35
Baum, M., 150, 162
Bean, K. L., 105
Beck, A. T., xix, xxvi
Becker, W. C., xv, xxvi
Bergin, A. B., xxvii, 162
Bernstein, D. A., 92
Bernstein, V. I., 53
Blanchard, E. B., 35
Borkovec, T. D., 92
Boulougouris, J. C., 35
Brady, J. P., 11, 17
Breger, L., xvii, xxvi
Burdock, E. I., xxvii
Bucher, B., xviii, xxvi, 135, 139

C

Cameron, R., 127
Cautela, J. R., xv, xx, xxvi, 42, 53, 66, 69, 77, 122, 127
Craighead, W. E., 139

D

Davidson, P. O., xxvi
DiScipio, W. J., xviii, xxvi

Dobson, W. R., 139
Donner, L., 152, 162
Drabman, R., xv, xxvii
Drenner, W., 92

E

Edwards, J. E., 53
Eisler, R., 35
Elkes, E., 162
Ellis, A., xv, xxvi, 125, 127
Eysenck, H. J., v-vii, 116, 117, 127, 143, 160, 162

F

Feld, S., xiii, xxvi
Feldman, M. P., 126, 127
Fenichel, O., 24, 35
Fensterheim, H., 77
Flint, A. A., 162
Folkins, C. H., 124, 127
Foppa, K., xvi, xxvi
Freud, S., xv
Friedman, R. M., xxvi

G

Gallman, W., 92
Garfield, S. L., xxvii, 162
Geer, J. H., xx, xxvi, 84, 91
Gelder, M. G., xx, xxvi, 23-24, 35, 105
Gelfand, D. M., 139
Gelfand, S., 139
Gericke, J. R., 46, 53
Gittelman, M., 124, 127
Glaser, R., xxvi
Graver, L., xix, xxvi
Grusec, J. E., 127
Guerney, G. G., Jr., 152, 162
Gurin, G., xiii, xxvi

165

SUBJECT INDEX

A

Agoraphobia, 5-17, 96, 98-99, *see also* Phobias

Alcoholism, xix, 59-62, 63, *see also* Drug abuse

Animal experiments, 149-151

Assertive training, 18, 43, 49-50, 63, 67, 74, 88-89, 100

Autism, 135

Automated therapy, 152, 158

Aversion relief, 30, 48, 86-88, 91, 120

Aversive conditioning, 34, 65, 72, 117, 118-122, 126-127, 135, 161

Avoidance conditioning, 48-49, 52, 72

B

Baseline, xvii, xxi, xxiv, 21, 41, 153-154, *see also* Behavior analysis; Reversal; Multiple baseline

Bedwetting, xix, xxi

Behavior Analysis, xvi, xvii, xxi, 8-10, 21-24, 39-42, 60-65, 82-84, 97-100, 113-117, 131-133, *see also* Baseline; Multiple baseline; Reversal designs

Behavior rehearsal, 73-74, 88, 89, 100, 101-102, 118, 158, *see also* Assertive training

Behavior shaping, 43-46, 52, 88, 101, 134-135, *see also* Successive approximation procedures

Behavioral model of behavior change, 143-149

Bender-Gestalt Test, 116

Booster sessions in behavior therapy, xxii, 121, 122, 126, 127

Brain damage, xix, 116

C

Cancer phobia, 21-22

Clinical inference, xiii, xiv

Clinical problem-solving, 145, 148

Clinical vs. actuarial assessment, 153-155

Cognitive behavior modification, xv, xviii, 30-31, 90, *see also* Cognitive rehearsal; Covert sensitization; Stress inoculation

Cognitive rehearsal, xviii, 12, 30

Compulsive hand washing, 20, 29, 32-33

Contingency contracting, 46

Contingency management, 44-53, 129, 158

Conversion hysteria, 78, 90

Covert sensitization, xviii, 66-67, 69-72, 118, 122-124, 161

D

Depression, xix, 59, 90, 115

Differential social reinforcement, 134-135

Discrimination learning, 87, 91, 120, 129

Drug abuse, xviii, xix, 59, 61-62, 65

Dyadic interaction patterns, 145-149

Dysmenorrhea, 37

E

Electroconvulsive therapy, 18, 50, 81

Environmental influence, xv, xvi, 144

Epilepsy, xix

Ethics, 113, 137

Exhibitionism, 110-112, 114-115, 126

Extinction, 25, 137, 145-150, *see also* Flooding

Eysenck Personality Inventory, 116

F

Fading, 134

Fear Survey Schedule, xx, 9, 10, 15, 23, 32, 41, 50, 64, 74-75, 84, 99, 116

Feedback, 99-100

169

Date Due